MURDER & MAYHEM
— IN —
BOISE

MARK IVERSON AND JEFF WADE

Published by The History Press
Charleston, SC
www.historypress.com

Copyright © 2022 by Mark Iverson and Jeff Wade
All rights reserved

Back cover: "Boise Flour Mills—Cyrus Jacobs Flour Mill & Brewery." *Jess A. Whitker Collection, Idaho State Archives.*

First published 2022

Manufactured in the United States

ISBN 9781467151696

Library of Congress Control Number: 2022937890

Notice: The information in this book is true and complete to the best of our knowledge. It is offered without guarantee on the part of the authors or The History Press. The authors and The History Press disclaim all liability in connection with the use of this book.

All rights reserved. No part of this book may be reproduced or transmitted in any form whatsoever without prior written permission from the publisher except in the case of brief quotations embodied in critical articles and reviews.

*I dedicate this book to my father, Gary Iverson,
whose love of history inspired me to follow my life's passion.*

—*Mark Iverson*

CONTENTS

Preface, by Jeff Wade ... 7
Acknowledgements ... 9
Introduction ... 11

Cemetery Stories: Where'd Dr. McIteeny Get To and the Sad Tale
    of Sergeant Peter Vogel ... 15
Ezekiel Litell's Axe to Grind ... 20
Grove Street Gutting ... 22
H.B. Lane Orders a Drink—Is Served a Shot ... 25
The Wheels of Justice Begin to Turn ... 28
Simeon Walters's Short Drop ... 32
A Bad Year in the Life of T. Burmester, Esquire ... 36
Never Let Your Guard Down at Goodwin's Mill ... 41
Prison Break!: A Shootout at the Old Pen Orchard ... 43
Boise's Avenging Angell ... 53
Who Was William L. Toomey? ... 57
Swept to Eternity by the Raging Waters of the Boise River ... 64
It's Not Always Good to Be King ... 67
The Butcher of Bannock Street ... 75
The Warm Plunge of Death ... 85
How Not to Clean a Stove ... 91
An Old Pioneer Meets a Modern Death ... 93
A Dark Day in the Capitol of Light ... 97

Contents

Going Up—All the Way to Heaven	100
Failure to Raise the Dead: The Strange Afterlife of Boise's Edith Peshak	105
The Other Eastman Fire	115
The Cat Hunt	118
Bibliography	121
About the Authors	128

PREFACE

A few years ago, Mark had an idea. After leading a few walking tours around Boise, he began receiving specific types of questions regarding some of the historic sites he passed on his walks. These questions often involved the morbid, lurid and macabre nature of Boise's past. He soon realized that people did not simply want to hear the standard version of Boise's history—they wanted something darker. He started digging. After a few months of research, he possessed enough content to stitch together a historical walking tour called A Macabre History of Boise: A Walking Tour. Residents of Boise, Idaho, and tourists began to attend the tour; it became more popular than Mark originally expected. The recipe included a bit of solid history and a touch of murder, with a pinch of vice and prostitution for good measure.

I first heard of Mark and his Macabre Boise tour when Angie Davis, a mutual friend, posted an ad for the event on social media. The idea of a macabre tour really appealed to me. It is the only walking tour I have ever paid to attend. Walking along the streets of Boise with Mark, I could see the passion he had for telling local stories. By the time the two-hour tour was over, Mark let it slip that he was looking for a business partner. I wanted to work with him but was not quite ready for the commitment. Over the course of the next few weeks, we kept talking. I joked at one point that when he was ready to write a book on the macabre history of Boise, I could help him out. Apparently, he took that joke seriously because here we are publishing *Murder & Mayhem in Boise* together.

Preface

It has been an interesting ride turning an expanded version of Mark's tour into a book. This publication has allowed us to expand the geographical scope of the subject matter, from a few blocks in downtown Boise to a large part of the Eastern Boise Valley. I have learned so much about the history of Boise from our research, and I hope that through these stories our readers might do the same. As historians, our main goal is to teach this history, and we have chosen a unique way to do so. Through stories of death and tragedy, we better understand the evolution Boise has gone through, while also reminding us of what Boise was and, perhaps, what it might be again. From Boise City's wild frontier mining days through to the modern era, we endeavored to contextualize the stories of the common, everyday people who lived, struggled, failed, succeeded and often died in Boise.

Since we based this book on Mark's historical tour, we thought it appropriate to bring a little aspect of a tour to the book. We have included "Where to See It" sections at the end of each story so readers may visit the places mentioned for themselves should they wish. We hope that our book works as a sort of self-guided tour of the sites where some of Boise's most macabre events occurred. We would like to caution the reader to respect the places from this book they may choose to visit. Please be sure to respect private and public property, along with those people who died there.

—Jeff Wade

ACKNOWLEDGEMENTS

First of all, and most importantly, we would like to thank our wives, Blair and Michala, for giving us their love and support throughout the writing of this book, as well as building IdaHistory. We would also like to thank Blair for her editing and formatting. Almost as important, we would like to thank the staff at the Idaho State Archives for helping us find and scan many of the images you will see in this book.

We would also like to thank Anthony Parry at the Old Idaho Penitentiary for allowing us to visit and photograph the Old Pen cemetery on that cold, blustery day, as well as Daniel Grundel at the Boise Arts and History Department for digging through cemetery records to find that one name—that needle in the haystack.

INTRODUCTION

From its humble beginnings as a collection of merchant tents set up to serve miners headed to the Boise Basin and travelers on the Oregon Trail, Boise and its citizens contended with violence, as did most other frontier settlements. Along with the many good and honest citizens who moved to Boise City, there were more than a few of the rougher elements mixed in. The frontier era was a time when horse thieves and road agents rode unchecked through the Boise Valley, and meeting one's demise at the end of a gun was nearly as likely as dying from a plethora of rampant diseases. In the eastern United States, the violent cataclysm of the Civil War was being fought, while in the Boise River Valley, several companies of soldiers entered the Boise Valley on June 28, 1863. The troops first camped on Government Island, the area now comprising much of Garden City just west of downtown Boise. Their commander, Major Pinckney Lugenbeel, began searching for the best location to establish a military camp, and from July 2 to July 4, 1863, the same days the future of the Union was being decided on the fields of Gettysburg, Pennsylvania, Lugenbeel selected the site on which to build Fort Boise. Yet, eastern battlefields were not the only locations where the Civil War was fought; the mines of the western United States played an equally important role in deciding the fate of the nation. To strengthen the Union's grip on these mines, Lincoln established the Idaho Territory on March 3, 1863, allowing his administration to continue to use its wealth to fuel the war effort. Divided between law-abiding Idahoans and outlaws, miners and those who would rob them, settlers and indigenous peoples and

Introduction

Major Pinkney Lugenbeel. *D 497-A, Idaho State Archives.*

pro-Confederate and pro-Union citizens, it makes sense that the Idaho Territory, Boise City included, witnessed high levels of violence from the start.

Gold was discovered on Orofino Creek, a tributary of the Clearwater River, in 1861. Idaho's first gold rush had begun. From there, prospectors and miners worked their way south, establishing towns like Florence, Warren and Elk City along the way. In response to a vague description of possible gold fields farther south offered by a member of the Bannock Tribe, a number of expeditions left Florence in the early spring of 1862. When the treasure hunters reached a natural basin nestled between mountains, they commenced prospecting, finding gold in their pans on August 2. Soon after their arrival, the party was attacked by a band of Shoshone and one of the leaders of the group, George Grimes, was killed by the creek that now bears his name. He was deposited in a prospect hole and then covered over by his fellow miners, and his marked grave still rests at the top of Grimes Pass.

The discovery of gold in the Boise Basin, north to northeast of the future site of Boise City, on August 2, 1862, led directly to the establishment of Fort Boise a year later. More precious metals were discovered in the Owyhee Mountains southwest of Boise City, as well as to the east in boomtowns such as Atlanta and Rocky Bar that next year. Miners increasingly became dependent on Boise for most of their supplies, including mining tools, food, guns, booze and women. Thus, in Boise City, many people knew how to defend themselves from the dangers on the frontier and often carried guns and knives, as well as a healthy resolve to kill in order to preserve their own lives. The line between killing in defense of one's life and murder often proved blurry in territorial Idaho. In a town full of miners, soldiers and prostitutes, where the presence of booze, money, women and guns prevailed, violence flourished.

A short eleven months after first discovering gold in the Boise Basin, Boise was platted on July 7, 1863. Outlaws and ruffians from all over the newly established Idaho Territory began to congregate there. One popular place for the now prolific criminal element to gather was the saloon of David Updyke. Like many others, Updyke made a small fortune in the

Introduction

Fort Boise, 1870. *1-57, Idaho State Archives.*

mines before coming to Boise to open his saloon, which was attached to his other business, a livery stable. Shortly after, the law-abiding citizens of Boise began to accuse Updyke of being chief of the outlaws, responsible for organizing much of the livestock rustling, stagecoach robberies and bogus gold dust production in the area. To the dismay of many good citizens, Updyke was elected sheriff in 1864, but soon after a vigilance committee was formed to keep the rogues in check. However, violent lives often conclude violently, and Updyke's end, as well as that of his criminal empire, proved as short as the noose he dangled from. His story testifies to how far rogues could climb in the corrupt atmosphere of early Boise City.

Once Boise City evolved beyond its volatile adolescence, it entered a period of prosperity upon receiving statehood on July 3, 1890. By the turn of the century, Boise was boasting electric lights, the first major geothermal heating system in the nation, an opulent natatorium filled with warm spring water that drew visitors from all over the region and an electric streetcar system that would soon link many towns in the Boise Valley. With its Wild West days firmly behind it, deaths in Boise often resulted from the mechanics of modernization. Many Boiseans continued to lose their lives to the gun during this era, but just as many were likely to die from stepping in front of a streetcar, getting into an automobile accident or drowning immersed in the warm waters of the natatorium.

In a town such as this, residents often turned to religion to offer comfort and provide answers to questions of life and death. That is why twenty-one Boiseans left town in 1933 to join a commune (some say cult), based in

Introduction

southeastern Utah, whose leader proclaimed that she could bring the dead back to life. One family, the Peshaks, moved to the Utah desert because they believed her. Just as strange and mysterious was the story of a man who walked into a Catholic church in Boise, only to die by suicide after ingesting cyanide pills just outside the confessional. The man's identity and motives still confound the populace forty years on. Perhaps one of the deadliest forms of violence in the history of Boise has been perpetrated by jealous lovers. One of the only recorded pistol duels in Boise's history settled a dispute between a covetous husband and the lover of a young damsel—both participants happened to be lawyers. A generation later, what could be called Boise's first mass shooting occurred when an Alaskan gold miner sought revenge against the young woman who stood him up, her lover and his family. Women committed violence as well—one of Boise's postmasters found this out for himself in the early 1900s—while in one notorious case of a love triangle gone wrong, a man fell prey to foul play at the hands of his wife and her new beau.

Whatever era you decide to study in Boise's history, murder and mayhem abound. Traditional histories tend to cut these stories from the chronology of events forming the historical narrative of Idaho's capital city, completely ignoring the people who lived through these nightmares. By studying how the unfortunate among the prosperous died, we gain an appreciation for the lives of those whose stories are often willfully removed from history's pages and thus forgotten. The stories of the murdered and maimed are the focus of this book. Many of the names mentioned in this work will be hard to find anywhere else, aside from in a few old newspapers and the etchings carved on their gravestones.

CEMETERY STORIES

Where'd Dr. McIteeny Get To and the Sad Tale of Sergeant Peter Vogel

Nestled in the foothills past Fort Boise and up Mountain Cove Road sits a quiet and isolated military cemetery, an aging monument from the era of westward expansion and settlement. Some residents of the cemetery endured the most ferocious fighting of the Civil War before traveling west. Others among the dead fought in the Mexican-American War, the "Indian Wars," the Spanish-American War and in the Philippines. The cemetery is hallowed ground, the final resting place for 252 soldiers, veterans, their families and civilians. However, this cemetery once sat in a different location, a spot ill-suited to house Boise's dead. The land, once belonging to the dead and now managed by the City of Boise Parks & Recreation, is currently covered by a holding pond, levy, walking path and a small dog run. Fort Boise's cemetery was, in actuality, three different cemeteries positioned next to one another, with the military cemetery linking to the Catholic and citizen graves, which in turn sat near a small Jewish burial ground. Several key issues led to the U.S. Army eventually moving the cemeteries in 1907.

Since 1863 and the fort's first burials, the flooding of Cottonwood Creek had been an issue. Loose stock roamed freely in the foothills, trampling the sagebrush and grave markers alike. Too many people were being buried in the citizen cemetery with little to no organization, and civilian authorities failed to create any registry recording the inhabitants of the public burial ground. Finally, the military authorities sought to turn the former cemetery into a new firing range in the spring of 1909. Because Morris Hill Cemetery

Fort Boise Military Cemetery sign. *IdaHistory Collection.*

had opened in 1882 and Boiseans had begun burying their dead on the Boise Bench, it was to Morris Hill in 1909 that many of the citizens buried next to the soldiers at the fort cemetery were moved. Some of the soldiers made the short trip to Morris Hill as well. Most of the remaining troops' and citizens' eternal slumber was disturbed when they were moved to the hillside above Mountain Cove Road, farther up the canyon above Fort Boise, where they remain today. Yet not all the graves were accounted for; they still likely lie below the ground at the previous location.

One of the earliest residents of the old Boise citizen's cemetery met his death in 1866. Dr. J.S. McIteeny was a popular and helpful denizen of Boise City, applying his expertise to bettering the health and lives of his fellow Boiseans during the first few years of the town's existence. On Monday, August 6, 1866, Dr. McIteeny and his horse crossed the Boise River on a small ferry several miles upriver in the early afternoon, heading to the south bank to tend to a patient. After finishing treatment, the good doctor attempted to return via a popular ford in the river that McIteeny was well acquainted with, according to many of those who knew him. At about 5:00 p.m. that day, riders on the north bank of the Boise River found McIteeny's horse dripping wet, but its rider was nowhere in sight. After searching both riverbanks, the party found the location where the horse entered the water; it was seventy yards below where the animal was found wandering. As darkness fell and with the doctor still missing, the search was called off for the night.

Two days later, Dr. McInteeny's corpse was found floating in "deep, still water" several hundred yards below the spot the horse entered the river on its return to Boise. The doctor left behind a wife and four small daughters, the eldest being just seven years old. Dr. McInteeny's mortal remains were buried in the citizen's cemetery next to the fort's burial ground on August 9, 1866. There he remained for more than two decades, even as Cottonwood Creek regularly flooded its banks during the spring thaw. An 1889 article noted that "a devastating flood came from the hills…and in its rage and power tore down the monument erected by friends to commemorate his memory and opening his grave bore his remains away as if to join his spirit in the place unknown and from whence none return." An article in the 1907 *Idaho Daily Statesman* speculated that the doctor's corpse must have floated down through town on its way to the banks of the Boise, as that was where Cottonwood Creek's flood waters exited the canyon, but no documents from 1889 substantiate this grisly claim. What is certain is that burying the citizens of Boise directly below the area's most active tributary creek proved a poor idea.

A WEATHERED MONOLITH POCKMARKED with bullet holes stands near the north entrance of the fort cemetery, a monument to four European immigrants and veterans. One of those memorialized is Sergeant Peter Vogel, a Civil War veteran who, after immigrating to Maine from the German Confederation of states in the 1850s, joined the First Battalion, Second U.S. Infantry, in 1862 at about twenty years old. He fought in twenty-seven separate engagements, including Second Bull Run, Antietam, Chancellorsville, Gettysburg and the Wilderness Campaign. After surviving the bloodiest battles of the war, Vogel reenlisted in the Second Battalion, Fourteenth Infantry, later renamed the Twenty-Third Infantry. As a professional soldier stationed out west, Vogel and his unit, Company H, engaged in the "Snake War" (the term "Snake Indians" was used by both soldiers and settlers to refer to the separate Northern Paiute, Bannock and Western Shoshone tribal bands that lived in the Snake River Basin). His commanding officers at Fort Boise praised Vogel's manner, calling him "one of the most upright, brave, sober and faithful soldiers the service has ever produced."

Peter Vogel headstone at Fort Boise Military Cemetery. *IdaHistory Collection.*

On the night of September 13, 1869, Sergeant Vogel followed orders to collect a group of soldiers out on the town causing a ruckus while at a local saloon and put an end to a specific dispute over a woman of the demimonde known to many as "drunken Jessie." Private Holden, one of the soldiers garrisoned at Fort Boise, felt sore that Jessie had shut the door to her room in his face with southern "gentleman" gambler William Tracy remaining within. The establishment was one "low and wretched den of infamy" among many in Boise, somewhere near the intersection of Eighth and Main. Upon forcefully entering Jessie's room, Vogel asked where Private Holden had gone off to. Tracy, rolling off of Jessie, yelled "Get out!" and fired off several shots before coldly stating, "I'm busy." Two rounds took effect and ended the sergeant's life. Different versions surrounding Vogel's murder quickly developed. Some witnesses testified that he had been shot in a premeditated killing because of Tracy's sympathies for the defeated Confederacy. Others swore that he died in defense of fellow soldiers as he burst into Jessie's room, where she had taken up with Tracy. What we can confirm is the good sergeant received two shots from the revolver of the southern gambler inside a bawdy house along Eighth Street where Tracy and "drunken Jessie" were in the midst of finalizing a "transaction." Vogel died later at a saloon on Main Street after having been carried there by his fellow soldiers.

Townspeople began to talk, and the word around town argued that the army had overstepped its mandate by intruding on William Tracy's "intimacies" with Jessie, especially because the incident occurred on private property. The *Idaho Tri-Weekly Statesman* reported that Tracy's bail was set at $3,000, a steep sum the defendant managed to pay. Eventually, a grand jury refused to indict Tracy for shooting Vogel, determining that he acted in self-defense. Upon Tracy's release, his friends advised him to flee town lest some of Vogel's comrades take vengeance. He heeded their advice, setting off for Utah soon after.

Thus perished Sergeant Peter Vogel, survivor of twenty-seven battles and engagements of the Civil War, at the business end of gentleman gambler William Tracy's revolver in a Boise City brothel, September 13, 1869.

Where to See It: Peter Vogel and his fellow soldiers are buried at the Fort Boise Military Cemetery within the Boise Foothills Military Reserve up Mountain Cove Road, just north of downtown. Keep driving up the road until you see the cemetery on the hillside just off the roadway to your left. The monolith sits on the far end of the cemetery near the second of the two entrances at the north end of the grounds. Sergeant Vogel is buried directly next to the monument where the hill begins to rise. He has no personal marker. Nothing is known of the whereabouts of Dr. McInteeny's remains, other than they no longer remained in the cemetery after the flood of 1889.

EZEKIEL LITELL'S AXE TO GRIND

Thomas Litell's other children warned their father not to release his twenty-six-year-old son, Ezekiel, from the Oregon State Asylum near Portland back in 1866 and that to take charge of Ezekiel's care would prove a major mistake. Their brother was incurably insane, they told their father. Recently, Ezekiel had begun threatening to kill his father, but as of yet, either out of lack of willpower or opportunity, he had not carried through with committing patricide. Despite his children's admonitions, Thomas and Ezekiel left Portland for William Litell's property in East Boise in the summer or fall of 1866. The Litell farm was located on either side of Hot Springs Road, known today as Warm Springs Avenue, directly south of where the Idaho Territorial Penitentiary would be constructed in 1870 and 1871. Having trekked west from Pennsylvania to Iowa, Iowa to Illinois and Illinois to Canyonville, Oregon, in 1860, the Litell clan split up in Oregon, and William resettled in Boise sometime after 1863. Besides maintaining a homestead, William owned a ferry crossing with his father where Moore's Creek flowed into the Boise River in the far eastern portion of the Boise Valley. The ferry occupied much of William's time, taking him away from the farm for much of the day if not longer. This often left Ezekiel alone with his father.

Perhaps Thomas believed that Ezekiel would in reality never hurt him—or maybe he simply failed to take the threat into consideration—but he let his guard down. On February 3, 1867, neighbor and orchardist Robert Wilson witnessed Ezekiel walking toward the Boise River shortly after "a little Indian boy, six or seven years old, who was living at Litell's, came over to Wilson's and said 'old man sick' 'old man dead.'" Wilson hurried over

Hawthorne Asylum, Portland, Oregon, circa 1872. *ID-26037, Oregon Historical Society.*

to William's house and found Thomas almost dead and splayed out on the floor with a deep gash in his head made by an axe then resting in a corner of the room. After being informed of the murder, Deputy Sherrif Thompson organized a manhunt in the area by the river, eventually finding Ezekiel camped on an island in the Boise River. He had lit a fire and started drying his clothes by the fire. Upon being arrested and taken to the scene of his crime, Ezekiel showed no emotion or reaction to his father's grisly death. He refused to answer questions relating to the crime before being taken to jail. Thomas was buried, and the question of what to do with Ezekiel fell to local authorities to arrange. Difficulties arose for officials, both in Portland and Boise City; neither municipality sought to take charge of the troubled man, and a conflict developed wherein Ezekiel was passed back and forth between the two cities for several years. However, by 1870, residency had been established for him at the Oregon State Asylum. Ezekiel grew old in Oregon, eventually moving to the capital city of Salem by 1895. He died in Lane County, Oregon, in 1915 at the age of seventy-three.

WHERE TO SEE IT: Nothing exists of William Litell's homestead once located between Hot Springs Road, now Warm Springs Avenue, and the Boise River. The western edge of Warm Springs Golf Course, then moving eastward, would once have made up a considerable portion of Litell's property.

GROVE STREET GUTTING

A jealous crime or the violent act of a deranged man? Sometimes the destructive actions of brutal men are left unexplained. This is certainly true of the murder of Joseph Craig in Boise City on Halloween night in 1870. The tragic tale began when Dr. Ephraim Smith, lying in bed in his comfortable home at the intersection of Tenth and Grove Streets, heard a *thud* on his front porch and a faint rapping at the door between ten and eleven o'clock in the evening. Upon opening the door, he found a grievously injured Joseph Craig desperately attempting to keep his entrails within his body. Upon taking Craig into the house and examining his wounds, Dr. Smith identified two major cuts across the stricken man's belly, each starting on opposite sides of his stomach and meeting nearly in the middle. The doctor later shared that it looked as if the man had been cut in two. After bandaging Craig's dreadful wounds to the best of his ability, Smith and a few others transported the patient to the house he boarded at on Eleventh Street between Idaho and Bannock Streets, the scene of the crime.

Earlier that evening, Joseph Craig, D.W. Blake and Mrs. Blake enjoyed dinner together, as often happened at the Blake household. The Blakes were comfortable around Craig because the young man had lived with them for the last few years at Loon Creek, Idaho, a mining region close to Leesburg, Idaho, a ghost town these days. From Loon Creek, the Blake family and Craig went to the region near Salmon, Idaho, for a few months before abandoning the area for Boise City in October 1870. Craig then purchased the land on which he would live with the Blakes; D.W. Blake got to work conducting odd jobs around town and chopping wood, and Craig began to work as a bartender at an unspecified saloon. Things were going well for the Blakes and Joseph Craig.

D.W. Blake, his wife would later state, had a sinister side to himself as well, along with a history of mental illness of an off-and-on-again nature. On their way from Iowa to Idaho, Mrs. Blake related how her husband had attempted to commit suicide on the trail and "would have accomplished his purpose had she not arrived in time to prevent it by pushing aside the gun." Since no one could rationalize why Blake ended up attacking his friend Craig, partial insanity was viewed as a good reason as any. On that Halloween night of 1870, after finishing supper and numerous drafts of whiskey, D.W., Mrs. Blake and Craig stayed up talking until just before ten o'clock in the evening, when D.W. went to bed, leaving the two others talking. The pair continued talking for ten minutes or so before Craig informed Mrs. Blake that he intended to be present for breakfast the next morning. She asked that he go fetch some fresh water from the pump outside so she had enough to make biscuits in the morning. He went outside and began to pump the water.

Dr. Ephraim Smith. *Idaho State Archives.*

After pumping the water, Joseph Craig returned to the outside step, where he met Mrs. Blake and handed her the water. At that moment, D.W. Blake came running out the door, shouting, "This is what you are up to!" As he yelled, he struck his friend in the stomach. Craig, startled and in pain, asked D.W. what he meant. D.W. replied with, "I'll show you what I mean," at which point he struck Craig in the stomach again. Mrs. Blake then noticed that her husband possessed a small pocket knife and took it from his grasp as he turned to attack her. While the wild and aggressive D.W. was disarmed, Craig realized that he was grievously injured, so much so that he began to stagger toward Dr. Smith's house at Tenth and Grove Streets. After the doctor attended to Craig and brought his patient home, he knew that the poor man was not long for the world. Craig died the next morning, on November 1, 1870.

While Joseph Craig lay dying at Dr. Smith's residence, D.W. Blake, while crying, told Mrs. Blake to take care of the children. He took some blankets and headed off toward the mountains, where Mrs. Blake guessed he had "gone out somewhere and taken his own life." This might have been the end of it, but five years later, the *Idaho Tri-Weekly Statesman* reported on December 27, 1875, that a Mary C. Blake had won custody of her children from D.W. Blake in court. Two of these children had been in their rooms with the windows open the night of Joseph Craig's murder; D.W.'s son had been ten then, and he witnessed it all. The cause of the attack most agreed on was that liquor and insanity got the best of D.W. Blake and that in a jealous fit of rage, he killed his close friend.

WHERE TO SEE IT: Dr. Smith's home once sat at the intersection of Tenth and Grove Streets on the western edge of downtown Boise. Nothing remains of the house where Joseph Craig came for medical assistance, nor the home where the young victim was stabbed and sliced open. It once sat midway between Idaho and Bannock Streets on Eleventh.

H.B. LANE ORDERS A DRINK—IS SERVED A SHOT

Louis Risely was a troubled man, addicted to drink and prone to moments of extreme delirium. His difficult circumstances and sickly condition were certainly worsened by working as a bartender at one of Boise City's earliest saloons, the Central, located on the north side of Main Street between Sixth and Seventh Streets. A son of Jacksonville, Illinois, Risely was described by the *Idaho Tri-Weekly Statesman* as "a man about twenty-eight years of age, and for two years or so a resident of this place" who "for several months past…has been in ill health." Additionally, the newspaper noted that Risely "was addicted to hard drinking, and in the last week had an attack of delirium tremens." After suffering a series of violent seizures due to his addiction, Risely informed his acquaintances that if he endured any more "attacks of the kind he should kill someone, and it would as likely be his nearest friends as any; that his 'head was not exactly right anyway.'" None of the people Risely confided in mentioned the afflicted man's threat to kill someone to any authority or person who might have acted to stop Risely's murderous plan before he carried it out.

By 1867, Boise City possessed the workings of a government. Among Boise's newly appointed officials were Judge Robert Gullespie and the young comptroller, H.B. Lane, whose office was situated downtown near Eighth and Main across from the Overland House, a popular stop for weary travelers on the Oregon Trail. Lane became a member of Boise's growing upper class and was a well-known, liked and important man around the town. H.B. Lane was acquainted with Louis Risely, and the

Main Street, 1866, from Fifth Street looking west. Visible at left are Sutler's Store and George Washington Stiles & Company blacksmiths. At right are the Wells Fargo office, The Brewery, a blacksmith's shop, the Stage House and the City Bakery sign. *ID-78-134-1, Idaho State Archives.*

two men considered each other friends. In the early morning hours of May 7, 1867, Judge Gullespie and Comptroller Lane sat down at the Central Saloon with a group of men playing whist, a popular card game during the nineteenth century. When Lane ordered a round for himself and the judge, Risely replied pleasantly and went to fetch the men their drinks—nothing hinting at a man well past the bounds of sanity. The barman was "seen to go from behind the bar to the corner of the billiard table and level a revolver at the persons sitting at the card table." Inexplicably to those on the scene, Risley fired into Lane's back as he attempted to rise from the table. He then took a shot at Judge Gillespie, who having been just missed by the bullet, ran for the door. Gillespie later described to reporters how, as he ran, he witnessed Risely point the revolver at his own head and fire. The judge recalled the ball taking effect, yet remarkably, the shot failed to kill or even drop Risely. Upon passing through the door to Seventh Street, present-day Capitol Boulevard, the judge shared seeing the stricken Lane lying prone on the ground, "having nearly breathed his last." As a group of men carried Lane into the Quivey & Graham Drug Store, Risely once again placed the gun against his head, his forehead to be exact, and shot

The whist party, 1861. *Library of Congress, Prints & Photographs Division, LC-2017647822.*

himself. He did not die immediately but suffered for half an hour before he expired. His victim died in the store into which he had been carried.

The citizens of Boise City were at a loss in trying to rationalize Risely's shooting of the innocent and beloved Comptroller Lane. Making matters more tragic was the fact that Lane was scheduled to be married several days after his death, but now his fiancée, whom the newspapers fail to name, ended up burying her husband-to-be instead. As a Mason, Lane was laid to rest with Masonic honors, although the Masons and Odd Fellows Cemetery, currently Boise's Pioneer Cemetery, would not be founded until 1872. Genealogist Wilda Collier Dillon maintains that Lane was laid to rest in the citizen's cemetery connected to Fort Boise's soldier cemetery; however, this cemetery was moved in 1907, with most citizens interred within being moved to Morris Hill Cemetery on the Boise Bench, founded in 1882. Neither Pioneer Cemetery nor Morris Hill nor the Fort Boise burial ground list H.B. Lane as being interred within the grounds. What we know for certain is that the affliction of the bottle resulted in many deaths, not just in Boise City but all over Idaho and the "Wild West" throughout the nineteenth century and beyond. A lack of understanding of the complexity of alcoholism combined with little sound knowledge concerning the challenges presented to those with mental health issues, along with the prevalence of firearms, created the environs in which the West became wild and deadly.

Where to Find It: The Central Saloon was once located where Boise City Hall now stands, on Main Street's north side.

THE WHEELS OF JUSTICE BEGIN TO TURN

As in many towns in the Wild West, human life often meant very little in early Boise City. One case that illustrates this sad fact is the story of a man who was killed in cold blood near the Payette River. When local papers reported the murder, the victim was simply referred to as a "Chinaman." Authorities offered no clues as to his identity or occupation. The initial motivation for murdering the Chinese man, the killer testified, was "just to try his hand at killing someone," although the murderer previously had plenty of opportunities to practice. The alleged killer was an Irish immigrant named Anthony McBride. He had immigrated to the United States around 1859, enlisting in the army a mere two years later, joining the Ninety-Ninth Pennsylvania Volunteer Infantry at the beginning of the Civil War. The Ninety-Ninth fought in some of the bloodiest battles of the war, including Second Bull Run, Fredericksburg and Gettysburg, where the regiment lost half of its number in combat. The Ninety-Ninth also witnessed General Lee surrender the Army of Northern Virginia at Appomattox and participated in the Grand Review of the Armies, a parade to honor the men who fought in the war, before a crowd still grieving the loss of President Lincoln in Washington, D.C.

The Ninety-Ninth Pennsylvania mustered out of service in July 1865, leaving Private McBride to look for a new occupation. He decided to join the Federal army, enlisting as a professional infantryman. He was assigned to the Fourteenth Infantry Regiment, Second Battalion, which traveled to California by ship via Panama and, from there, overland to Fort Vancouver before heading on to Fort Boise, Idaho Territory. Company C, to which McBride was assigned, received orders to man Camp Lyon on the Oregon and Idaho border near Jordan Valley to relieve volunteers from Oregon protecting the stage roads in the vicinity. Company C found itself in the heart of the Snake War, fighting several skirmishes with Paiute raiders in its first month at the camp. When not on patrol, the soldiers at Camp Lyon often drank heavily, making discipline a major issue. Perhaps not a fan of the poor living conditions in the camp, McBride deserted his post on April 17, 1866, finding work in the mines around the Boise and Weiser Valleys.

More than a year later, in August 1867, McBride was walking along the Payette River near Wieser when he came across two people sleeping in blankets on the riverbank. He asked in the nearby camp if the sleeping men were "Indians." When the men in the camp replied that they were not, McBride walked over to the riverbank, pulled his revolver and shot one of the pair in cold blood. McBride threatened witnesses that if they did anything, he would shoot them too. He demanded help in tossing the body into the river, but instead, bystanders took McBride into custody and

Camp Lyon, Idaho, March 3, 1870. *ID-62-212-2, Idaho State Archives.*

turned him over to the law. While riding the stage to Boise to face a judge, he remarked that he wished he had killed the witnesses.

Standing in front of Justice Gilepsie, McBride pleaded not guilty to the murder charge. The magistrate bound him over for trial and remanded him into the custody of the city jail. Of course, if enlisting in the army had failed to sequester the man, neither could a frontier jailhouse. McBride's jailers permitted their prisoner a walk down from his cell to the yard without shackles while the guard locked up the anteroom. When the guard made it down to the yard, McBride had disappeared. He was seen running toward the river and probably concealed himself among the willows. Sheriff Duval sent men out in all directions to find the escaped man, offering $100 for his capture. He was recaptured and placed back in jail awaiting trial.

McBride was found guilty of the killing and sentenced to death. During sentencing, McBride told the judge that it was another man who shot the victim and then ran away. This statement conflicted with his previous statements and witness accounts made in reference to the coldblooded killing. Not a single piece of mitigating evidence or testimony was presented in McBride's defense. The judge ordered him to be in close confinement in jail until the sentence was carried out. In custody, he shared living quarters with four other men, including two declared legally insane. One of the insane prisoners was Ezekiel Litell, jailed for killing his father with an axe. McBride seemed cheerful during his last days, joking around with his cellmates. He spent most of his time with a rosary in hand, counting the beads like any good Irish Catholic.

On January 24, 1868, McBride was moved from the jail about two miles out of town to the head of Crane Gulch. There, he was led to the platform where he would breathe his last. The prevailing consensus in Boise City at the time was that the sentence would not actually be carried out because it seemed no one could be punished for murder in Idaho Territory. However, some three hundred men had gathered, standing around the gallows constructed for the purpose of seeing the wheels of justice finally start to turn. McBride remained calm as he walked up the steps, showing little emotion. Father Cazeau had been chosen as his spiritual advisor. The priest uttered a short prayer as McBride faced the people who would watch him die.

When given a chance to address the crowd, McBride told those assembled that he had been drunk when he committed the crime and that he thought, at the time, that the man he killed was a "wild Indian." Even though his statements proved his guilt, he closed by claiming that he was innocent. As the

Anthony McBride desertion record. *National Archives and Records Administration (NARA), Washington, D.C.; Returns from Regular Army Infantry Regiments, June 1821–December 1916; Microfilm Serial: M665; Roll: 154.*

executioner fitted the noose, McBride was heard to exclaim, "By god, they've got me now!" He then looked at a soldier in the crowd and nodded, saying, "Goodbye Sergeant, we are not on the Truckee now." As the hood dropped over his face, his last words on this earth were, "Goodbye, gentlemen, all." When the trap was sprung, McBride made a clean drop, with not a twitch visible after. Just prior to his first enlistment in the Pennsylvania Volunteers, McBride had married Elizabeth Tower, a widow with eight children. He kept correspondence with her until around the time he deserted Camp Lyon. He told the *Idaho Statesman* reporter that he had not heard from Elizabeth since. In 1890, she claimed his Civil War pension.

McBride's execution proved to be the first "legal" hanging in southern Idaho, as well as the first in the territory since Howard, Lowrey and Romain were hanged in Lewiston in 1864 for killing poor Lloyd Magruder. When McBride hit the end of the rope, a sliver of confidence in the legitimate justice system began to build, and the era of vigilante justice in Idaho finally began to give way to legal trials dependent on courtrooms and judges.

WHERE TO SEE IT: Anthony McBride was launched into eternity between Bogus Basin Road and West Highland Drive at Parkhill Drive.

SIMEON WALTERS'S SHORT DROP

With his feet on the trap and a noose waiting nearby, Simeon Walters knew that he had no chance of reprieve. About fifteen minutes to two o'clock in the afternoon, on the tenth day of December 1869, the undersheriff stood in front of Walters and read his death warrant out loud. When given the opportunity to share any last words, Walters required the comfort of two priests standing by his side; he proclaimed his innocence for the last time, and a final prayer was uttered. A cap was placed over Walters's head, the straps securing his feet and hands were checked and he was left standing alone on the gallows. The sheriff stood, pocket watch in one hand and lever in the other, waiting for two o'clock to strike. When the hand struck two, he pushed the lever and then walked home while Walters fell into history.

More than a year before his date with the noose, Walters was working on a ranch north of Silver City in partnership with Joseph L. Bacon. Bacon decided to sell his share of the ranch to Walters, necessitating a trip to Boise City to complete the paperwork for the sale. On the agreed-on day, Walters found Bacon helping drive cattle for another rancher about twenty miles from Silver City. Bacon attempted to delay the trip, but Walters insisted that they leave. An argument ensued, but a compromise was reached wherein they would stay the night and set off the next morning.

At Walters's trial, several witnesses recalled seeing the two men in a buggy traveling north on the stage road toward Boise City. About one mile north of Fivemile Creek, an ox team driver named Kifer, also making his way

Silver City Road stage stop. *Annie Laurie Bird Collection, Idaho State Archives.*

to Boise City, reported being passed by Walters alone in a buggy. Roughly thirty minutes later, Walters came back in Kifer's direction and asked if Kifer had seen a six-shooter laying on the road anywhere; he had taken it out to shoot something a mile or so back and lost it, Walters reported. Kifer replied that he had not seen a gun, and Walters responded that the dust on the road would probably prevent him from finding it. He then turned his buggy around once more in the direction of Boise City.

That afternoon, Walters arrived at J.D. Agnew's livery stable on the corner of Eighth and Idaho. Agnew took charge of the buggy and horses, but a short time later, he witnessed Walters cleaning dust, or more likely evidence of a crime, from the buggy. Agnew told Walters not to worry about cleaning it, as washing the buggy was Agnew's job. Walters responded that the buggy required no washing, as he worried the paint might be ruined. Walters then retrieved a gun belt from the buggy, the U.S. Army cap box on the belt being so distinctive Agnew was able to identify it later in court. Witnesses from Silver City confirmed that the gun belt had belonged to Joe Bacon.

Walters sold the gun and belt, asking the gunsmith to reload two empty chambers in Walter's own six-shooter. He next went to Roth's general store, where he bought some items and asked if he might store his trunk at the business for safekeeping. The trunk belonged to Bacon, it turned out; it contained a photograph of his wife along with important paperwork, including the deed to the ranch. The following day, Walters arrived back at the ranch near Silver City, deed in hand, claiming that he left Bacon in Boise City. He was spotted on horseback later, riding toward Boise City once more when a stage driver saw him in the area of Fivemile Creek. He was next spotted in the area of Fruit's Ferry on the Snake River, which later came to be known as Walter's Ferry. He again returned to Bacon's former property, where he demanded the ranch hand give him possession of the land. The hand refused, telling Walters that until he received an order from Bacon, he would not comply. Walters allegedly replied, "I can't get that now." Suspicion started brewing, and Bacon's friends began to search for evidence that the rancher had been murdered.

Upon searching the stage road, they came upon Bacon's hat stuffed down into a badger hole. The searchers located buggy tracks leading off the road where the stage road crossed Fivemile Creek. Following the tracks,

Ferry on Snake River. *Annie Laurie Bird Collection, Idaho State Archives.*

the searchers found the location where the buggy had been stopped, some footprints and the imprint of a body on the ground. After identifying dried blood, they raced to Boise City, where they delivered the evidence to officers of the law, who issued a warrant for Walters's arrest. Another search of the area yielded the boots Bacon wore when he was attacked in addition to more tracks leading to the Snake River. Walters was arrested, and a grand jury charged him with first-degree murder.

A month and a half after Bacon went missing, the body of a man was found on the banks of the Snake River about twenty-five miles from Fruit's Ferry. Animals had eaten most of the flesh away from the body, and two bullet holes could be seen in the unfortunate man's skull, indicating that the victim had been shot in the back of the head, execution style. The body was positively identified when Bacon's glass eye was found nearby.

The prosecution presented the theory that Walters shot Bacon while they were riding in the buggy together. Walters had been seen by witnesses driving the wagon on the left side, an unusual way to drive the buggy. He likely did so in order to take advantage of Bacon's lack of vision on that side. Pulling his pistol without being observed, he shot the poor old rancher. He then pulled the wagon off the road to a small island in Fivemile Creek, where the stream crossed the stage road, and hid the body. On the return trip, he moved the body to the Snake River and disposed of it. The defense placed Walters on the stand, but under cross-examination, his story fell apart. During the closing remarks of the trial, the only argument Walters's attorney mustered was that the prosecution lacked a solid case.

The jury returned a verdict of guilty on the charge of first-degree murder before requesting that the judge show leniency in sentencing Walters. Unfortunately, the law allowed only for a sentence of death. All legal appeals failed, making Walters the first man to die at the hands of the Idaho territorial government in southern Idaho.

WHERE TO SEE IT: The place where Joe Bacon is believed to have been killed is now located on South Cole Road, just north of Boise Fire Station No. 17. Fivemile Creek passes underneath South Cole, which was the route of the old stage road. Walters was hanged at the Territorial Jail in Idaho City, Idaho.

A BAD YEAR IN THE LIFE OF T. BURMESTER, ESQUIRE

The year 1869 started off well for Theodore and Minnie Burmester. As a well-respected attorney and socialite in Boise City, Theodore involved himself in the local Democratic Party and the railroad committee and "had a long-established character for probity and honesty." In fact, he was of such high character that he refused to run for political office even when his friends snuck his name onto the ticket for city treasurer without his knowledge. Arminta "Minnie" Burmester was also well liked by those who knew her; she was referred to as a "most exemplary woman, a true and devoted wife, an admirably good mother, a true friend....She had the courage and strength of a heroine."

The Burmesters homesteaded a ranch about seven miles west of Boise City. Minnie minded the home and ranch while Theodore was away on business, as he was on May 18, 1869. Two hired hands worked the Burmesters' land: a Bohemian-born Romani man named John Konopeck and a Mr. Bevens. Konopeck was a Civil War veteran, and newspapers indicate that he was with Sherman during his destructive March to the Sea, while service records list him as a member of the Sixth Regiment of the Wisconsin Infantry. He had been wounded and briefly taken prisoner on the first day of the Battle of Gettysburg on July 1, 1863.

In May 1869, Konopeck and Mr. Bevens had been working the fields alongside the Burmesters' eldest child when Konopeck took his leave and headed toward the house. Upon encountering Minnie, he informed her he had cut his hand before asking for a rag. Minnie went into her bedroom to find a bandage kept in the bottom drawer of her dresser. Taking advantage of her kind and trusting nature, Konopeck attacked the unsuspecting woman while she was bent over. The implication in the newspapers at the time was that this was an attempted rape, but Minnie fought back against her attacker, leaving her bloody and exhausted from the fight. Konopeck left the room and went upstairs to retrieve his revolver.

Minnie, with a strong presence of mind, locked her door and retrieved a shotgun. When Konopeck came back downstairs, he fired two shots through the door but missed the young woman. He then went outside and looked into the room through the window. Minnie leveled the shotgun and pulled the trigger, but the gun failed to discharge. Konopeck fired three more shots at Minnie through the window, striking her once in the abdomen. She fell to the floor, unmoving.

Konopeck, probably assuming her dead, reentered the house to set fire to the structure. Minnie heard two final shots and the body of her would-be rapist hitting the floor of the kitchen. Minnie was able to drag herself from the burning farmhouse in time to see Mr. Bevens pulling a wagon full of brush away from the home. Apparently, at some point during the attack, Konopeck placed Burmester's one-year-old son, William, atop the wagon's brush pile. Mr. Bevens's quick action saved little Willie's life and kept the fire from spreading beyond the house.

After saving the child, Mr. Bevens attempted to enter the house to search for Minnie, but the flames frustrated his attempt at rescue. Circling around the house, he found Minnie near the road, and he quickly loaded her into the wagon and took her to the nearest ranch, that of Mr. Bixby. Messengers were sent to find Theodore, who arrived shortly before Minnie passed away, but not before giving her testimony of the incident. She was buried two days later, and her funeral was said to have been the largest in the territory at the time. The story of the tragedy was reprinted in newspapers as far away as England.

By the time he had buried his young wife, Theodore Burmester's bad year was but halfway over. He sent his two boys to live with his mother in Oregon while he focused on work at his law firm. One case he accepted was that of Mrs. Amanda Morford. Amanda's husband, Russell Morford, was also an attorney, but he had fallen on hard times—most likely caused by his drinking and gambling addictions. Burmester took pity on Morford and allowed him to share his room at a boardinghouse in Boise City. After a short time, Morford asked Burmester to help him reconcile with Amanda, introducing them. The three would be seen together discussing the matter, but soon rumors began to fly around town about Burmester and Amanda Morford—tales of midnight buggy rides with trips out to the Burmester ranch alone and Burmester's practice of paying a laborer to keep Morford sitting at the card table a little longer so he and Amanda could use the time together.

The tension came to a head when Amanda made the decision to hire Burmester to represent her in the divorce suit. John Hailey—whose résumé included work in ranching and mining, as a stage line operator, as a congressional delegate, as a territorial prison warden and as a historian, as well as being an eponym of the city of Hailey—warned her not to hire Burmester. His advice was to hire a married attorney or an old codger, anyone but the young handsome widower. If she did hire Burmester, Hailey warned, the whole affair would end badly.

John Hailey. *Library of Congress.*

One afternoon, while Hailey was standing on the porch of the home Amanda was staying at, Morford arrived. Just as Morford walked through the front door, he saw Burmester enter through the side door. Knowing that an altercation would ensue, Hailey decided to go in and wait to see what happened. He did not have to wait long, for almost immediately Burmester walked out of the house. Amanda told Morford that their marriage was over, and she was proceeding with the divorce. Morford replied, telling her that he would shoot any man she intended to marry with a double-barreled shotgun. Burmester heard this whole exchange.

A few days later, Hailey and Burmester were again at the home where Amanda resided when the proprietor of the house lost patience with Morford. Morford was yelling at Burmester when the owner told him to leave. Morford put his hand on his gun. The proprietor warned Morford that he would shoot him if he brought it out. As Burmester also reached for his piece, Hailey's voice boomed over the scene. "If there is any shooting done, I will take a hand in it myself," he warned the three men. A crisis had been averted for the moment.

On November 7, tensions between the two men finally came to a head. Morford and a friend from out of town went walking east of Boise City. Burmester and law partner S.P. Scanicker had also decided on a walk and

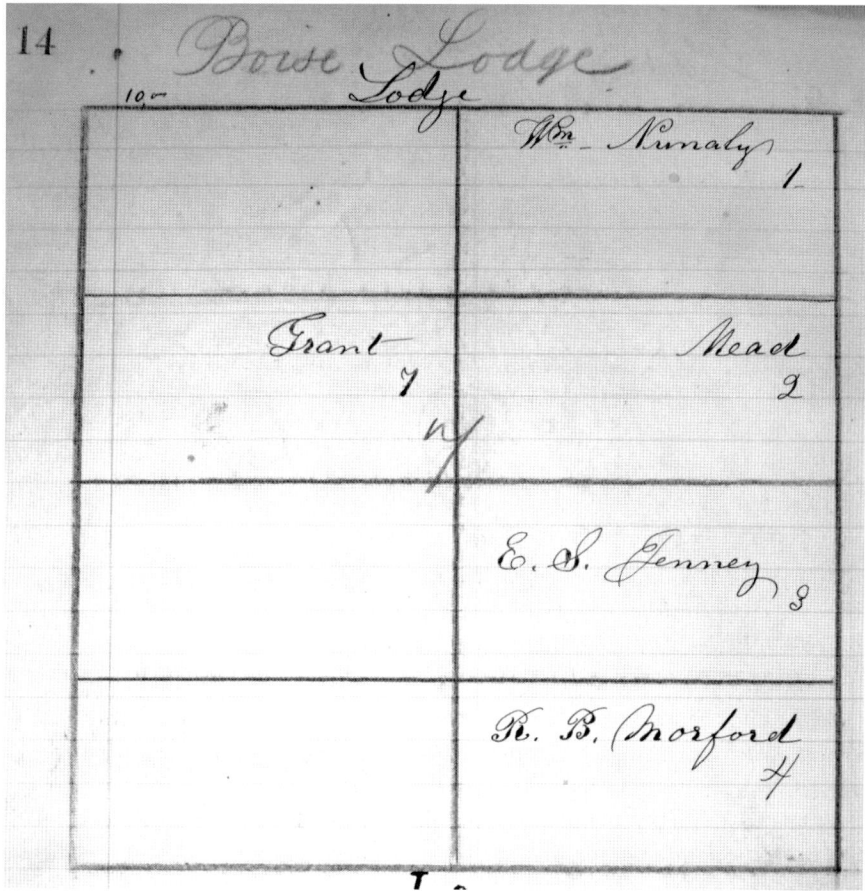

Masonic and Odd Fellows Cemetery (Pioneer Cemetery) lot plat map. *Boise City Department of Arts and History.*

headed in the same direction. Morford and his friend had turned around and were heading back toward town when they passed Burmester and Scanicker at a distance of about twenty paces. Burmester, apparently in response to some gesture of Morford's, said, "What do you mean by that?" Morford replied, "I mean you are a dirty rat." With that, both men pulled their sidearms and began firing.

Depending on which witness accounts you read, Morford fired two or three shots, while Burmester achieved three. When the smoke cleared, Morford was down—Burmester's third shot took effect in the man's right temple. The mortally wounded man was hauled back to town in J.D. Agnew's wagon; he lingered a day before finally expiring. In lieu of a divorce decree, officials handed Amanda a death certificate. The affair was a duel in all but name, although the newspapers refused to refer to it as such, perhaps as a way to shield the embryonic city from a violent reputation.

Burmester was arrested, and his trial was held in Idaho City, starting a day after Simeon Walters had been executed there. After a sensational trial with a witness list that included the editors of both the *Idaho Tri-Weekly Statesman* and the *Idaho World*, as well as John Hailey and other prominent early Boisieans, Burmester was acquitted—despite what many believed to be an attempt by the judge to sway the jury into finding the defendant guilty. The *Statesman* and the *Idaho World*, as they usually did, used their platforms to argue back and forth on the verdict for weeks. Burmester left Idaho, traveling to his mother's residence in Oregon and eventually settling in Utah. He remarried and named his daughter from his new marriage after his first wife. Amanda eventually remarried and died in Columbus, Ohio, in 1894. Russell Morford was buried in an unmarked grave at the Pioneer Cemetery in Boise.

WHERE TO SEE IT: The Burmester Ranch was located south of Highway 44, between Arney Lane and North Ulmer Lane. Russell Morford's unmarked grave is at the Pioneer Cemetery. The gunfight between Morford and Burmester occurred somewhere near East Main Street and First Street.

NEVER LET YOUR GUARD DOWN AT GOODWIN'S MILL

Sawmills are filled with many potential mechanisms that can cause any number of horrific deaths. These mills proved particularly hazardous during the early days of western expansion in southern Idaho, a time when lumber was in high demand as towns, particularly Boise City, steadily grew and miners flooded the area in search of gold and other precious metals. Goodwin's Mill was one such place that once sat at the eastern end of today's Warm Springs Avenue, just east of Warm Springs Golf Course on the Boise River. Although Goodwin's maintained a predominantly safe record, a few tragic and messy events hung over its reputation like a dark cloud. Although A.G. Marion, another proprietor of the sawmill, recalled a businessman by the name of Clark constructing a mill on the site in 1864, the business maintained the name Goodwin's Mill, named after owner and operator Moses Hubbard Goodwin, after the entrepreneur purchased the operation in the late 1870s. Regardless of ownership, Goodwin's held a respectable safety record until November 29, 1893, when a young man named Elmer Morrison made a mistake while operating a large saw. A brief article in the *Idaho Daily Statesman* describes how Elmer "stooped down and put his hand on the fast revolving saw to test it's [*sic*] heat when his coat was caught by the teeth and he was drawn into its deadly grasp." Additionally, the paper notes that "the saw cut off one-third of his shoulder blade, one-half of his collar bone and took off one-half of the humerus." Elmer also received a serious gash on the skull measuring sixteen inches in length. In an effort to save his life, doctors amputated the remainder of his arm at the

Goodwin's Mill and crew. *Hugh Hartman.*

shoulder joint. Unsurprisingly, the injured lumberman died of his injuries, leaving his wife and two children without a husband and father.

Elmer's tragic accident would not be the last time a deadly mistake would be made at the sawmill. A.G. Marion recalled the dangerous confidence of an "experienced loader," the individual responsible for loading and unloading timber and lumber for wagons, train cars and truck beds. One afternoon, while unloading a pile of logs into Goodwin Mill's pond, a large number of logs got stuck and would not separate after the chains were removed from the stack. Noticing that the loader continued to try and loosen the pile, Marion said that he "yelled at him not to take any chances," to which the loader replied that "it was safe and that he knew what he was doing." He walked to the car on which the logs rested and employed a hook to dislodge the pile when, as Marion had warned, it came crashing down on him, killing him instantly. The logging industry was dangerous to many of those employed in harvesting, transporting and processing wood so that it might be transformed into lumber. Trees easily fell on loggers, men riding log booms down the Boise and Payette Rivers often drowned or were crushed by large floating logs and men were mangled by machines with sharp points and cutting blades. To simply manufacture the lumber that would build Boise City and many other towns, a fee paid in sweat and blood was owed the reaper.

WHERE TO SEE IT: Goodwin's Mill once sat at the east end of Warm Springs Golf Course in East Boise. Along the Boise River Greenbelt, an interpretive sign points out the mill's location.

PRISON BREAK!

A Shootout at the Old Pen Orchard

Before Warm Springs became Boise's most luxurious avenue, it was a well-tread wagon road leading weary travelers to or away from town, with locals calling it "Old Hot Springs Road." After 1872, the original gray walls of Boise's Old Penitentiary loomed menacingly in the near distance, buttressed by the foothills within view of those traveling the road. Nearer the roadway sat the orchard of Robert Wilson, who partnered with the prison in a mutually beneficial association; the prisoners picked the fruit for the prison, and Wilson made some money. These specifically chosen inmates were, supposedly, the nonviolent types. The lucky convicts received the designation of trustee, meaning they could work in the open among the trees in the orchard outside the prison walls. However, a handful of these special trustees proved supremely untrustworthy.

On Thursday, September 23, 1880, prison guard and warden J.S. White of the Idaho Territorial Penitentiary rode hard down Old Hot Springs Road to Boise City followed by one fellow guard and Mr. Cutting Clark, who owned a homestead near the prison. After witnessing White's furious ride into town, a crowd quickly formed. The breathless rider informed anyone within earshot that six prisoners had escaped, acquired guns and were at that moment holed up in Robert Wilson's house in the orchard near the penitentiary. Almost immediately, a posse of townsfolk assembled. U.S. Marshal Chase and famed lawman Colonel Rube Robbins led the hastily assembled group east toward Wilson's orchard. As the group traveled toward

Idaho State Penitentiary, 1945. *Idaho State Historical Society, 72-64-3c, Idaho State Old Penitentiary Collection.*

the shootout, the men met a detachment of soldiers led by a Lieutenant Galbraith, coming from Fort Boise to assist the guards.

The crisis started earlier that afternoon when a group of trustees had been picking and cutting fruit near Wilson's house, located across the coach road from the penitentiary just north of the Boise City Canal. The inmates had been under the supervision of Warden J.S. White. At a prearranged time, one of six prisoners signaled to the other five, prompting inmate William Mays and four others to rush White. Having secured the disoriented guard, the inmates stole two revolvers and ran toward Wilson's house with White in tow. They surprised Robert Wilson and his employee, who had been investigating the commotion; the inmates took the men hostage and entered the orchardist's home. Yet many years later, in 1941, an *Idaho Statesman* reporter interviewed Mrs. Wilson and daughter Nellie about life on the old orchard during Boise's early years, and Robert's widow recalled the event slightly differently. During her interview, Mrs. Wilson recalled her husband running to sound the alarm while the escaped convicts burst into the cabin and forced her to tell them where her husband kept his heavy tools. However, the article from the *Idaho Tri-Weekly Statesman* on September 25, 1880, described Wilson being abducted and taken into his own home. Regardless of the discrepancy, once inside the home, the convicts appropriated two breech-loading shotguns and a belt of cartridges, readying themselves for the coming fight.

Of the six prisoners involved in the plot to escape from the orchard, five had secured themselves in Wilson's cabin. William Woods, the sixth plotter, wisely decided to sit out the escape attempt, walking back to his prison cell while the others attacked Warden White. Both William Mays and William H. Overholtz were serving life sentences for robbing the U.S. mail, while William F. Reese (aka William Trent) earned ten years for robbing Middleton's post office. Finally, Maroni Hicks and John Wilson owed the

Robert Wilson House. *ID-1975-2-48, Idaho State Archives.*

Boise Canal water wheel. *IdaHistory Collection.*

citizens of the Idaho Territory ten years apiece for manslaughter. Inside the house, as the five prisoners desperately tried to free themselves from their shackles, Robert Wilson, his employee and White snuck away. Mrs. Wilson sounded the alarm, while Warden White gathered a posse. However, in Mrs. Wilson's interview for the *Idaho Statesman* in 1941, she stated that it was her husband who sounded the alarm. Regardless, one of the Wilsons reported the escape in progress to some men working at Clark's Mill, a short distance to the east. They, in turn, alerted guard G.W. Newman of the emergency as he supervised a convict labor crew working on the hillside behind the pen. Coincidentally, several soldiers on their way back to Fort Boise had been passing the mill as the alarm sounded, hastening Newman to race the prisoners back inside the prison before he hurried to meet the soldiers. Together, the four men rushed to Wilson's orchard.

As guard Newman and the three soldiers closed in on the house, they remained unaware that the convicts inside possessed firearms. When Newman approached the front of the house, he received a shotgun blast to the face; then, upon turning his horse around, he sustained another burst of shot to his back. Severely wounded and unable to properly see, Newman retreated from the fight and would, miraculously, survive and heal from his wounds. By this time, the three remaining soldiers had been joined by Marshal Chase, Warden White, Colonel Robbins and the posse, as well as the detachment of soldiers coming from Fort Boise. They proceeded to direct their collective fire on the house. Despite the poor odds, the convicts put up a stiff fight, shooting Corporal Coppage of Company F, First Cavalry, in the chest and severely wounding the unlucky soldier. Coppage also survived. The skirmish did not go all the outlaws' way, however, and soon William Reese, age twenty, received a mortal wound—a shot from a powerful long-range carbine—in the back, through his bowels, exiting his body about a half inch below the navel. Later, Reese was taken back to his cell, where he died under the care of his friend and cellmate William Woods. On his deathbed, Reese, who in actuality was not Reese at all, confessed that he had been born William Trent in Manitou, Utah, and that his parents were wealthy people whose well-known name he wished not to besmirch. He also confessed that Woods and John Wilson had nothing to do with accosting Warden White. He died at 4:00 a.m. on Friday, September 24, 1880. On the base of his tombstone in the prison cemetery, an unknown individual scratched "Reese" into the stone below his legal name.

At some point during the gunfight, the four prisoners worked their way out of Wilson's home from the rear of the building facing the Boise River. The

Grave of W.M. Trent. *ID-73-229-2-hhh, Idaho State Archives.*

authorities originally believed that William Mays, William H. Overholtz and Maroni Hicks had forded the Boise before heading south toward the Snake River. John Wilson, they determined, chose to break off from the group and head west down the Boise's northern bank. Additionally, Boisean James Flanigan noticed his horse missing from his property and alerted the authorities, who found the horse wandering three miles downriver from town. Wilson, the marshal thought, most likely stole a faster horse before making a bid to reach Walla Walla, in the Washington Territory, where he lived prior to his imprisonment. Marshal Chase, his posse and the contingent of soldiers from Fort Boise followed the trail of the three escaped convicts south, chasing the men that Thursday night until their horses could go no farther. Upon returning to Boise, the marshal secured a new mount, six fresh soldiers and several helpful citizens, and the new

Left: William Trent headstone at the Old Idaho Penitentiary Cemetery. *IdaHistory Collection*.

Below: Robert Wilson House, 2022. *IdaHistory Collection*.

posse rode out to Dunn's Station, a well-known rest stop for stagecoaches traveling the Overland Road. Circumstances changed, however, after evidence was found in the vicinity of the penitentiary suggesting the three convicts remained in the area.

In the early morning hours on Friday, September 24, 1880, guards on duty at the penitentiary heard a knock on the main gate and, upon asking who was there without reply, speculated that it had been the escaped convicts attempting to trick the guards into opening the gate so they might kill the guards and release their fellow prisoners. The next morning, upon searching the hills above the prison, guards found fresh chain and shackle tracks around the prison quarry. Tools were also missing from the quarry, suggesting that not every prisoner had succeeded in freeing themselves of his bonds. Additionally, near their friend and fellow convict William Reese's recently occupied grave, similar tracks were identified. Investigators soon found more footprints leading to a spot on the Boise River's north bank, directly across from a river island just south of Robert Wilson's place. After an uncomfortable few nights hiding on the island, the convicts moved upriver, eventually making their way past Idaho City and up to Willow Creek, about forty miles northeast of Boise.

Now above Idaho City, the prisoners came upon the camp of hunter James McQuat and friends on Willow Creek. They laid in wait. After returning to camp that evening, hunters R.B. Reed and John Wilson, a completely different Wilson than the convict, prepared supper and began to eat when they saw five men approaching their camp. Assuming it was McQuat and his company, they were easily surprised and captured by the prisoners, who had already seized McQuat. The convicts tied the group of hunters up before eating their fill of the men's dinner. After their unearned and hearty repast, the inmates took the hunters' rifles, horses and provisions before leaving the men tied up at the mercy of the elements. Reinvigorated and reequipped, the convicts headed southeast toward Rattlesnake Station, a stage stop between Boise and Glenns Ferry situated on the Snake River. At Glenns Ferry, the three prisoners—William Mays, William Overholtz and Maroni Hicks—broke into ferryman Glenn's cellar and stole some canned oysters and salmon. Seeing that his cellar had been robbed, Glenn himself tracked the convicts three miles east along the Snake River and, upon coming to a small slough extending from the river, sighted the men on an island with his belongings, including clothes and other provisions.

J.S. White and four other men followed Glenn's trail, adding twenty additional miles to it, until they reached the Bliss family home several miles north of the Snake River. On October 14, J.S. White had written to Colonel Robbins in Boise, sharing the news that he and three men had come upon the prisoners encamped among the rocks and sage in the area of the Malad River the previous day. White described the confrontation, stating that "we saw all three of them and drove them back into their camp at the mouth of the Malade [sic]." After cornering the escapees, White related, "we gave it to them hot and heavy, but did not succeed in hitting either of them." The convicts attempted to gain altitude and any type of advantage, as White noted how "there was a fierce climbing through the sagebrush," and "the convicts had their guns to their shoulders, but did not fire: why I cannot tell." White speculated that he and his posse would be forced to kill Mays and Overholtz before the chase concluded but that Hicks would then give up. As far as food, they had little, except for the cans they had stolen from Glenn, not amounting to much, and some ox meat they stole. White believed that the criminals were running out of options and suffered from low morale.

Eventually, J.S. White's posse turned around and headed back to Boise, while White acquired the help of a young man from the area named Doc Decker. The two men relocated the prisoners' trail running some twenty miles up Clover Creek to a spot hidden in the rocks and sage. White and Decker retreated to the Bliss house and welcome news. Waiting at the home for White to return were George Froman and Neil Harlett, two deputies sent by U.S. Marshal Chase to assist White. After journeying twenty miles up Clover Creek once more, the men found the prisoners' campsite abandoned. It appeared that the prisoners had been traveling at night and lying low during daylight hours. Over the next several nights, the lawmen hid among the scruff and scrag hoping to ambush the outlaws, but they did not succeed. Finally, just above the mouth of the Malad River, White and Decker spotted Hicks looking toward the hills in their direction without spotting them. They crawled through the brush to the top of a cliff just above the convicts. The lawmen appeared just in time to see Hicks and Mays attempting to ford the river. However, the current was far too strong, and the desperate men turned around. White and Decker remained hidden for the next several hours awaiting the prisoners' departure from their camp, which sat about twenty-five yards away from the lawmen. Froman and Harlett stationed themselves far above White's position, attempting to trap the convicts between two fields of fire. At some point, the convicts attempted to move, but coming under heavy fire from Froman and Harlett, they turned toward White's position— he, too, began to fire. As it grew dark and began to rain, the already soaked

Malad Gorge. *Idaho State Parks, Department of Parks and Recreation.*

prisoners retreated down the Malad River to a previous camp. The posse returned to the Bliss home to wait out the weather.

The next day, early in the morning, the lawmen started out fresh following the escapees' trail. The officers figured that the convicts had to be running out of the will to continue, as they had no food, were wet and had gone weeks without proper sleep. Several times that day, the posse cornered the prisoners, but eventually the convicts found a bridge and sought to cross the Malad. White and his men later tactically retreated and took up at a homestead named Payne's Ranch, where they waited for the desperate men to seek shelter and provisions. The prisoners crossed the bridge and found their way to a potato patch, where they harvested themselves raw spuds to fill their bellies. The game of cat and mouse continued around Payne's Ranch for nearly a week before the lawmen spotted a light among the sage and rock about two thousand yards off from Payne's house one night. After creeping stealthily into sight of the prisoners' camp, they saw that in a desperate bid to cook their food, the convicts had lit a fire, risking being caught by the dogged lawmen hot on their tracks. The hunters opened fire on their quarry. In a rush to flee the corral they camped in, the prisoners knocked one another over in the attempt to reach the guns they so carelessly cast aside when thinking mostly of their stomachs. The outlaws, it became clear, were not getting away. As bullets and buckshot whistled all around them, Overholtz placed his hat on a pole and held it above his head, indicating that the outlaws wanted to talk. Froman urged them to surrender, and after they reassured the convicts that they were the law and not vigilante cattlemen looking to hang the prisoners for stealing their cattle, the inmates surrendered. After turning themselves over, it became evident immediately that the prisoners were emaciated. Furthermore, Hicks was seriously ill. Back within the secure stone walls of the Idaho Territorial Penitentiary, a bed and warm food, even in a prison, proved welcome relief to Mays, Overholtz and Hicks.

An article in the *Idaho Semi-Weekly World* dated October 29, 1880, celebrated the capture of Mays, Overholtz and Hicks but also mentioned that John Wilson had still not been apprehended. Mysteriously, several years later, on July 17, 1884, the *Idaho Tri-Weekly Statesman* reprinted a story originally appearing in the *Walla Walla Union* on July 12 titled "A Bad Egg"; it described a rough-looking man in Walla Walla, in the Washington Territory, dressed "in an old ill-fitting suit of black broadcloth," having been placed under police surveillance. When a police officer named Robinson witnessed the man bumming drinks and money off citizens, he ordered him to leave town. The man appealed to Walla Walla's mayor but found little sympathy. Shortly after the mysterious drifter left town, Officer Robinson realized that he was, in actuality, Mr. James Lucy, aliases Wilson and Marshall, a convict on the run with a seventy-five-dollar reward on his head. The description of the wanted man being five feet and eleven inches tall, with grayish-blue eyes and about thirty-nine years old resembled that of John Wilson as described in the *Idaho Tri-Weekly Statesman* four years earlier. What became of the man—Lucy, Wilson or Marshall—remains a mystery.

WHERE TO SEE IT: Robert Wilson's house still stands in its original location. Although the structure has been modified over the years, the original frame of the building remains and is punctuated by the original middle window facing the property's front lawn. Wilson's old house is a private residence located on Bob's Drive, a small lane that runs from Warm Springs Avenue on the right side of the road headed east. The grave of William Trent, alias William Reese, can be visited at the Idaho Botanical Gardens next to the Old Idaho Penitentiary at 2445 Old Penitentiary Road in Boise. Trent originally rested under the south wall of the prison where the botanical garden is located. Special permission from the botanical gardens is required to visit the prison cemetery.

BOISE'S AVENGING ANGELL

Instead of a parcel or letter, a six-shooter and a club are what Alice Angell carried into Boise City's Post Office in early January 1884. Her target was the postmaster, a preacher named Jeremiah McKean. As he was alerted to her presence by the clerk, McKean was able to wrestle the pistol from the angry woman's hand before she could discharge it, but she got in a few good whacks with the club before she was turned away. Alice, like many other women in the West at the time, was a strong lady, not one to be trifled with. She was a pioneer who, having been born in Ohio, had traveled to California, where she met and married her first husband, William Angell, in 1861. William and Alice had three children together, and the family moved to Silver City, where William became a probate judge. When William died in 1879, Alice moved to Boise. After her attack on Postmaster McKean, she published a card, a brief statement, in the *Boise Democrat* to partially explain the incident:

> A Card—A desire to unmask a hypocrite, who, under the robes of a minister of God is serving the Devil, as well as to correct and set at rest the many conflicting rumors no doubt in circulation, combined with the hope that the truth told may be the means of preventing the unwary from falling victims to the duplicity of a villian, induce me to make public the following statement: Rev. Jeremiah McKean, postmaster at Boise City, while under the sacred promise of marriage to me, is also under a like promise to another lady. That in order to more effectually conceal his perfidy from both, he

so contrived by smooth and deceitful talk, that one should not meet the other. That suspecting his double-dealing, I obtained an interview with the other lady, who stated without reserve that she also was under promise of marriage to the reverend gentleman. The foregoing is the solemn truth, and I leave the public to form its own estimate of the character of the man who stands guilty of so base conduct. How many others he has deceived in like manner, who, through timidity, have been forced to silence, may never be known.

Mrs. Alice S. Angell
Boise City, Jan. 14, 1884.

The other woman to whom Jeremiah allegedly promised himself is never named, but he had just gotten divorced two months before the incident at the post office. Nothing is known about his first wife, Almeda, or the reason why they separated. Perhaps she was the other woman Alice mentioned, or maybe Almeda found out about Alice or the other woman. Either way, Jeremiah deserved a few good smacks from a heavy club at the least. His tenure as postmaster would only last a few more months before he went back to preaching. When he passed away in Monroe, Washington, in 1920, he was a respected banker. When the *Idaho Statesman* reported his death, a story was also included recounting a tale from Jeremiah's days preaching during the Boise Basin gold rush. A drunken ruffian continually interrupted his sermon, so the preacher removed his frock, went into the congregation, grabbed the heckler and threw him out into the road. When the drunk recovered enough to square up on Jeremiah, the preacher delivered an uppercut and ended any fight the ruffian had left in him.

After she ditched the reverend, Alice's life got much better. Five months later, she married another Boise Basin pioneer named Isham L. Tiner. He was a Mexican-American War veteran who came out west to mine in California in 1851. When news of Idaho gold strikes reached him, he sold off his interests and entered the Boise Basin with $1,500 to his name. He then found a successful claim to purchase. He mined near Placerville for two years, pulling out $200 per week in gold dust. In 1863, he moved to Boise City, where he bought six acres of land for fruit orchards. Isham would go on to obtain several properties in the Boise Valley during his life, including a chunk of Boise between Eighth and Tenth Streets at Fort Street. Known as the Tiner Tract, this 350-foot-by-640-foot plot was considered for the state capitol building. Alice owned a building located at 1010 Main Street, known

Above: The Averyl-Tiner Building (in the center of the photo). *IdaHistory Collection*.

Left: Alice Angell illustration. *From the* Illustrated Police News *(Boston)*.

as the Averyl or Tiner Building, the location of the Hotel Manitou. Isham served a term as Ada County sheriff and became warden of the Idaho Penitentiary for a short time. Later in life, the Tiners were both involved in the Historical Society for Idaho Pioneers. Alice passed away in 1912. Isham followed her three years later.

Back in 1884, Alice's post office maneuver gained her a bit of notoriety. Her card regarding McKean was reprinted in a few newspapers, and you can be sure that everyone in town was talking about it. Her story also appeared in the February 16, 1884 edition of the *Illustrated Police News*, a weekly magazine from Boston that reported sensational news of crime from all over the United States. The illustration attached to the story shows McKean grabbing the gun in Alice's hand as the club is cocked back above her head, ready to strike a vengeful blow on the head of her former lover.

WHERE TO SEE IT: In 1884, the Boise Post Office was located on Main Street between Seventh and Eighth Streets. The Tiner Building still stands at 1010 Main Street.

WHO WAS WILLIAM L. TOOMEY?

It was a balmy early December evening when Grace Leeburn was getting ready for evening mass at the Sacred Heart Church, located at 811 South Latah Street in Boise. Grace's husband was something of a local celebrity and war hero. Lieutenant Colonel Leo J. Leeburn started his career as a pilot in World War I and worked his way up to the commander of the army air base at Gowen Field just outside Boise during the Second World War. As such, the Leeburns were often called on to host visiting dignitaries. There was no way for her to know, as she traveled to church that evening, but on December 4, 1982, she would become involved in a mystery that one day would be even more well known than her husband.

The evening mass was scheduled to begin at 6:00 p.m., but one man had arrived early to the chapel. He likely hoped to give his confession to the parish priest before the service began, but upon his arrival, he found the confessional already occupied, so he sat down in a nearby pew. When Grace Leeburn entered the chapel to prepare for mass, she found the man there, except he was not sitting now—he was on the floor, not moving and not breathing. Grace alerted her son, Leo Jr., the head usher. Leo fetched another parishioner, a registered nurse named Virginia Almquist. She went right to work but found that the man had no pulse and was rigid and cold. At first, the now numerous parishioners assumed the man was a member of their church, but they soon realized that no one recognized him. He was a stranger to all of them.

Sacred Heart Catholic Church. *IdaHistory Collection.*

The police arrived a short time later, while church leaders directed arriving parishioners to the church's gym, where mass was held while Boise police detective Frank Richardson started his investigation. He dug through the man's pockets, expecting to find a driver's license or identification card or anything else with the man's name on it. Instead, Detective Richardson found a note folded around nineteen $100 bills. The note was typewritten and read, "In the event of my death, the enclosed currency should give more than adequate compensation for my funeral or disposal (preferred to be cremated) expenditures. What is left over, please take this as a contribution to this church. God will see to your honesty in this." The note was signed "Wm. L. Toomey."

When the police tried to find Toomey's family to notify them of his death, no one living in the Boise area with that name. As they widened their search, they lifted fingerprints from the corpse and sent them off to the Idaho Crime Bureau and the Federal Bureau of Investigation. Neither database was able to provide a clue to the man's real identity. Striking out everywhere else they looked, the police turned to the mystery man's appearance for clues to identify him.

Toomey sketch. *Boise Police Department.*

The dead man was wearing a Seiko wristwatch, blue jeans, a green western-style long-sleeve shirt and a bolo tie. The best clue taken from his clothing was his belt, which had a $100 Mexican peso coin set into the belt buckle. On the back of the buckle was the name "P. White," which was later traced to an artist in Phoenix, Arizona. The man was white, thirty-five to forty-five years old, 175 pounds and six feet tall, with a dark tan and light colored, possibly sun-bleached hair. A tan and sun-bleached hair did not seem normal for someone in December in Boise, Idaho. The man's appearance led investigators to believe that Toomey was from or had recently visited the southwestern United States. Investigators suspected that the name Toomey was an alias, and it so happened that R.J. Toomey is the name of a company from Boston that manufactures ceremonial clothing for Catholic priests.

While the police searched for Toomey's actual identity, the coroner's office was searching for a cause of death. Upon finding Toomey, the cause of death was initially inconclusive but suspected as poisoning from a caustic substance. Chief Deputy Coroner Erwin Sonnenberg removed a substance from the body and sent it to the lab. When the lab results came back, his suspicion was confirmed: Toomey died from cyanide poisoning, which prompted his death to be ruled a suicide. At the time, cyanide was easily obtainable, and the year Toomey died was the same year seven people were murdered with Tylenol laced with the poison. Since Toomey could not be identified, his body had to be buried instead of cremated per his note. The money he left was seized by the county, and he was buried in a pauper's grave at the Syringa Garden Cemetery, now part of Dry Creek Cemetery, with a simple stone marker with the name "Toomey" scratched into it. The taxpayers were billed $600 for the burial.

The members of the Sacred Heart Church did what they could to honor the mystery man. When the body was released by the coroner, they were allowed to hold a funeral for Toomey on December 27. The priest of the church, Reverend W. Thomas Faucher, chose to use the ceremony to honor everyone who died in despair during the holidays, including three other people who died from suicide in Boise. While standing beside Toomey's stark gray casket, Father Faucher told the 150 people gathered in the

The grave of William Toomey at Dry Creek Cemetery, Boise, Idaho. *IdaHistory Collection.*

Garden of Prayer Plaque at Sacred Heart Catholic Church. *IdaHistory Collection.*

church, "He came to us to die. We don't know who he is, but we come here in faith, to pray for him—whoever he may be, and to pray for ourselves." The church members who found Toomey—Grace and Leo Leeburn Jr., Virginia Almquist and Father Faucher—participated in an episode of the television show *Unsolved Mysteries* that aired on March 21, 1990. In that episode, Faucher presented the theory that Toomey was a Catholic and that he came to Sacred Heart to kill himself "in a fashion that somehow or another made his peace with God....I think somewhere deep within him was a very religious spirit." To further honor the unknown man, the church placed a plaque in its prayer garden reading, "The Garden of Prayer Given by the Leeburn Family, Mr. Oral Andrews, and an Unknown Wanderer."

Just because Toomey's body was buried did not mean that the search for his identity was over, especially for Detective Richardson. He told the *Idaho Statesman*, "I'm sure someone is looking for him. For what, I don't know." Eleven years after Toomey's death, Richardson was watching the news television show *A Current Affair*, which was covering the case of Juan Reyos, who was convicted of murdering a Catholic priest named Father Patrick Ryan. Reyos and his supporters pointed to the fact that he was being issued a speeding ticket some two hundred miles from the murder scene at the time Father Ryan was beaten to death in a West Texas hotel room on December 21, 1981. On August 7, 1982, Father Reynaldo Rivera was shot to death after being lured to a rest stop in Santa Fe, New Mexico. Another priest, Father Ben Carrier, was found murdered in his Yuma, Arizona hotel room on November 10, 1982, and his killing remains unsolved.

When Detective Richardson first heard of these priest murders from the Southwest, he could not shake the feeling that the man calling himself William L. Toomey had been involved. Police suspected from the beginning that Toomey was from the Southwest, where all three of these murders took place, all within a year of when Toomey walked into the Sacred Heart Church to kill himself. Richardson began a quest to finally identify Boise's John Doe and perhaps connect him with the priest murders. He contacted two journalists who shared the same goals. The trio tried again to match Toomey's fingerprints, but when the search came up empty again, they concluded that Toomey had never committed a crime, been in the military or had a job that required a professional license—all of which made Richardson and his team suspect that Toomey may have been a Catholic priest himself or even the victim of sexual abuse by one. Fathers Ryan and Carrier were both suspected of having lured young men into their hotel rooms for sexual encounters, and it is thought that they were both killed during one of these incidents.

During this time, it was a common practice of the Catholic Church to move priests accused of sexual misconduct from parish to parish instead of removing them from service. With this knowledge, the team of investigators began trying to ask the Catholic Church to help them identify William Toomey. Letters with requests for church leaders to look at the sketch of Toomey were ignored. They returned to Boise, where they went back to the Sacred Heart Church and sat down with Father W. Thomas Faucher, the priest who officiated Toomey's funeral; he was still the head priest of the church. "All we got out of him when we confronted him with our suspicions was a big, old grin."

Detective Frank Richardson passed away from cancer in June 2019, about eight months after members of the Boise Police Department raided a home owned by the Catholic Church Diocese in northwest Boise. There the police found thousands of images depicting heinous sexual acts against children, videos of animals being sexually assaulted and killed and what prosecutors called, "an actual snuff film" of a woman being raped and murdered. On the computers in the home, they found e-mails with these images, and chat logs discussing vile acts such as sexually assaulting altar boys and plans to travel to South America to abduct children to rape and murder. The resident of the home, W. Thomas Faucher, now retired, was arrested and charged with ten counts of sexual exploitation of a child and one count of possession of a controlled substance, LSD. The investigation began with a tip to the National Center for Missing and Exploited Children and turned into the worst case ever investigated by Idaho's Internet Crimes Against Children Task Force.

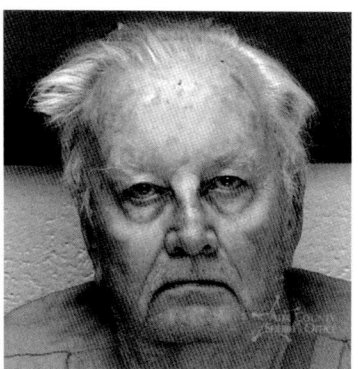

W. Thomas Faucher mugshot. *Sheriff's Department of Ada County.*

Faucher pleaded guilty to several child pornography charges, was given a fixed sentence of twenty-five years and was moved to the Idaho State Correctional Institution. On October 30, 2020, Faucher was found unresponsive and was declared dead at 10:52 a.m. Sadly, Faucher was not the only priest at Sacred Heart to be accused of heinous things. Father James McSorley, who immediately preceded Faucher at the church, has been accused of molesting one of the church's altar boys. His accuser alleges that McSorley gave him beer to keep the then twelve-year-old boy quiet. When the young man reported the abuse to the diocese, McSorley was moved to another church, prompting Faucher's arrival. McSorley had previously bounced around to different churches around the Pacific Northwest, likely because he had abused other children. Strangely, while Faucher was in jail awaiting trial, he began speaking out about how the Boise Diocese covered up many such accusations and called for church leaders to publish the names of every priest who has been accused of sexual misdeeds.

To this day, the identity of William L. Toomey is one of the most enduring and intriguing mysteries in the history of Boise. In a July 10, 2020 interview with *Variety* magazine, Tracey Dunn Meuer, creator and producer of *Unsolved Mysteries*, mentioned that the Toomey case could soon be solved by investigators working for the police department, yet in an e-mail, the Boise Police Department denied that any of its personnel are working on it. It is possible, however, that a private investigator is on the case. This is a mystery that seems solvable, yet an answer has eluded authorities and internet detectives for four decades. It is possible that the identity of Toomey may soon be revealed, but it seems more likely that the truth died with W. Thomas Faucher.

Where to See It: Sacred Heart Church is still an active church at 811 South Latah Street, Boise, Idaho. Toomey's grave can be found at the west end of Dry Creek Cemetery in Section 2S, Block 62, Lot 2-S. Although it is hard to find on the internet, the *Unsolved Mysteries* episode featuring Toomey is the twenty-third episode from the second season.

SWEPT TO ETERNITY BY THE RAGING WATERS OF THE BOISE RIVER

Residents and visitors to Boise alike often seek a walk along the Greenbelt to enjoy a little peace and solitude in the middle of a growing metropolis. Walking along the Greenbelt path near Ninth Street, trail users will come across a bridge located at an idyllic location to stop and snap photos of the waters of the Boise River rushing below. Back in 1864, a ferry built by John McLlellen and William Thompson began operating at this section of the river to move people and goods from Boise City to South Boise. McLellen's Ferry operated until a bridge, built by flour mill owner H.P. Isaacs, was completed in January 1868. For decades, the Boise City Bridge, later known as both the Ninth Street Bridge and Eighth Street Bridge, was the only way to get across the river without getting wet.

At this same spot, what had started off as a beautiful late spring day along the Boise River for Nellie Stephenson turned into one of abject terror and absolute tragedy. Most days, Nellie would hitch up their old gray horse to the family buggy, load up her four-year-old son, Jimmy, and then pick up fourteen-year-old Tommy Watkins from his home. Tommy would usually accompany Nellie and Jimmy on their daily buggy rides through town, helping out with the boy when Nellie had stops to make. On June 3, 1903, the trio was returning to the Stephenson home at 822 Thatcher from South Boise when they came to the Ninth Street Bridge. The bridge, then being around thirty-five years old, was due to be closed for repairs the following week; a pile of lumber had been placed by the northern end of the bridge to replace the old, rotted rails. According to the accounts of several witnesses on the bridge, Nellie's buggy reached a point about halfway across the bridge when the horse spotted the pile of lumber and was spooked. The old gray horse began to back up, which caused the buggy to jackknife, the rear wheels being pushed against the rail on the east side of the bridge meant to keep people and vehicles from accidentally going into the river. No matter what she did, Nellie could not convince the horse to stop backing up. As Nellie jumped out of the buggy to try to gain control of the horse by grabbing hold of the bridle reins, the animal took another step backward and the rail broke with a loud *crack*. The rail-board, buggy, horse and children dropped into the river below.

When they heard the horse balk and boards began to crack, several men and a twelve-year-old boy rushed to try to help, but all were too late. The group watched in horror, keeping Nellie from jumping in as the river swept the boys away. The flooding river rushed by at an estimated eight to ten miles per hour, making any rescue attempt impossible. The last time the boys were seen alive, they were on the west side of the bridge, with Tommy holding tight to Jimmy as they swept by. The buggy could be seen for a while longer, but the boys were gone.

Nellie was escorted from the scene of the accident to her husband James's office in the Sonna Building, located at Ninth and Main. James Stephenson was assistant to the state of Idaho's engineer; the bridge his only son died

Ninth Street Bridge as it appeared in July 2009. *Larry D. Moore, CC BY-SA 3.0.*

on was maintained by Ada County. Sadly, his job involved the building and repair of state bridges. As the Boise chief of police and Ada County sheriff organized a search, word passed to Tommy's parents. Moses Watkins, Tommy's father, flew into a fit of rage and grief, casting aside several men who attempted to restrain him. Eventually, he was placed in the county jail with his wife's consent until he was calm enough to be released. The horse and buggy were found the next day, but the two boys could not be found. The search continued, and the Elks Club offered a $125 reward per boy.

Several weeks later, Moses Watkins had a premonition that he would find his boy, so on the morning of June 21, he set out looking. He started at the Ninth Street Bridge and then slowly worked his way downriver. By this time, the river had fallen several feet to its normal summertime level, exposing several sandbars and small islands. On one of these islands near the railroad bridge, about one mile downriver from the bridge, Moses saw a human form protruding from the sand. He waded through the shallow stream to where he could see a head and arm. As Moses started to pull his son out of the bed of the river, several spectators watching from the riverbank waded over to help, while another ran to inform Mrs. Watkins of the recovery. Tommy's clothes were recognized, and the funeral was held that evening due to the advanced state of decay of the body. Even without a public notice, a large crowd gathered at Morris Hill Cemetery to support the family. Moses was awarded $125 from the Elks lodge for recovering the body of his own son. Sadly, little Jimmy was never found.

WHERE TO SEE IT: The Ninth Street Bridge is now a footbridge on the Greenbelt between Ninth Street and South Capitol Boulevard, just south of the Anne Frank Human Rights Memorial.

IT'S NOT ALWAYS GOOD TO BE KING

In 1913, a scandal rocked the Boise Police Department. Gambling, prostitution and the illicit sale of liquor had become all too common in Boise City, and the city's law enforcement seemed unable or unwilling to do anything about it. When asked why the patrol officers did nothing, they said it was the detective division's responsibility. The detectives pointed the blame back at the uniformed officers.

Mayor Arthur Hodges made a statement, spreading the word that Boise was "wide open" to gamblers and vowing to fight vice even if he had to replace all of his police officers "top to bottom." The man who took the blame was Detective Captain Dave Rich, who had previously served as a deputy sheriff, game warden and, most recently, deputy warden of the penitentiary. The city attorney accused Captain Rich and his detectives of allowing vice to run rampant in Boise and sent charges of dereliction of duties to the city council. It was claimed that many under Captain Rich's command "have been influenced by a disreputable character…who is alleged to have been consulted in the action of the detective department."

As the city attorney prepared his case against Captain Rich, he found that many of the witnesses he wanted to interview had simply disappeared from the city, probably loaded on the train and sent away. Rumors began to swirl that a crime boss known as "King of the Tenderloin" was asking questions of certain city officials to find out the extent of the charges—this being the same man who had been influencing Captain Rich's enforcement, or lack thereof, of the gambling and other vice laws in the city.

On Monday, January 20, 1913, the city council held a hearing on the charge against Captain Rich. During the course of the proceedings, it was revealed that the King of the Tenderloin was a man named Doc Sheehan. The hearing on the charge of dereliction of duty was little more than a kangaroo court, having no legal authority to convict anyone of criminal charges. This was especially evident when Rich's attorney objected to a particular statement from a witness. His objection was overruled by the mayor, who stated that they would hear any evidence of gambling in the city and would not be bound by the legal rules of evidence. The bulk of the prosecution's evidence was hearsay and focused on Rich's interactions with Sheehan. Several witnesses had spotted Rich and Sheehan together on many occasions. However, the council voted to acquit Captain Rich of wrongdoing. Instead, it passed an ordinance to join the detectives and uniform police under one department, with the chief of police being in charge of both divisions. Despite the offer for Captain Rich to maintain his position as detective captain, he turned in his badge and resigned from the city police force.

According to his inmate file from the Idaho Penitentiary, James Adrian "Doc" Sheehan was born in Port Townsend, Washington, on October 19, 1871. His father was John C. Sheehan, who served as sheriff. At nineteen years old, James left Port Townsend, reportedly owing $500 in bills. The newspaper mentioned that "cards, wine, and women were the cause." On November 15, 1895, he was arrested and charged with grand larceny for stealing a gold watch worth $30. When it was later revealed that the watch was not worth that much, the charges were dropped, and Sheehan decided to head north to British Columbia, where he would shortly thereafter have another run-in with the law.

He settled in Stevenston, near Vancouver, where he gained work as a bartender and rented a house that had recently been vacated by a man named Tosh McKenzie, who had a reputation for being a disreputable character. McKenzie, after having been banished from Stevenston for his many ill deeds, came back to town to find Sheehan living in his house. McKenzie ordered Sheehan out, and the two got into a scuffle. McKenzie pulled his revolver, but Sheehan was faster, shooting McKenzie in the face. The bullet traveled upward through the bad man's brain, and McKenzie fell dead. After a few court hearings, Sheehan was acquitted of willful murder.

Sheehan's next stop was Portland, where in 1903 he was arrested for taking $40 from a pair of young tourists during a game of bunco. For this crime, he was sentenced to three years in the Oregon State Penitentiary. He returned to Portland after his release but was arrested for vagrancy in 1907 just because he was an ex-convict. Despite this obvious railroading by the police, when he went to court, the judge was just as unkind. During his initial appearance, the judge supposedly saw Sheehan wink at a group of six other vagrants in the courtroom. The judge thought this might be some kind of signal and remanded Sheehan into custody, but the charge was later dropped, eyelid movement notwithstanding. He made it to Montana, where he did a short stretch at the state prison in Deer Lodge for swindling a man out of a large sum of money over a card game. He was also rumored to have been involved in a gold dust robbery from the steamship *Humboldt*. While the ship was en route from Alaska to Seattle, $575,000 worth of the precious metal went missing in 1910. Already a professional thief and fraudster, he would have found Boise ripe for the taking.

After the police department controversy of 1913, Doc Sheehan retained his title of King of Boise's Tenderloin and the police department stayed corrupt. That November, Captain George Smith was also forced to resign after being accused of frequenting a bawdy house owned by "negress" Belle Murray. Sheehan's Starling Hotel was just one of several buildings Doc Sheehan would come to own in the red-light district, many of which were on Main Street between Seventh and Eighth Streets. The back side of these buildings was the infamous Levy's Alley, a place where prostitution and crime ran unchecked for decades.

On December 9, 1913, Sheehan's Starling Hotel was the site of a double tragedy. Thomas Brown, a contractor from Caldwell, and Fred Wallace (or Wallis), a laborer from a nearby camp, were found dead in their beds after a night of drunken partying. The coroner immediately suspected that the two men had died from drug overdoses, either from morphine or cocaine, which was becoming quite popular as a party drug in Boise at the time.

The year 1914 brought even more controversy to Doc Sheehan's life. On Monday, March 2, at around 3:30 a.m., a fire broke out at 724½ Main Street, spread to 722½ Main Street and also damaged the Owl Drug Store, which was below 724½. The investigation showed that the fire was clearly arson, as the firebug had attempted to set fires in three different locations in the building before successfully lighting a blaze under the stairs. The building in which the fire started was owned by Sheehan but occupied by a former demimonde and housemistress named Ruby Vaughn. Ruby had moved out of the building just a few days before, taking her personal belongings but leaving furniture behind that she still owed money on.

The Starling Hotel, at left. *Idaho State Archives, 74-157-7.*

Shortly after the fire, Sheehan sued Vaughn for unpaid rent in the amount of $150. In her response, Vaughn claimed that she paid every penny of that amount and made some pretty harsh allegations against Sheehan. She started by mentioning that Sheehan was aware that the property was used for illicit activities while she was renting, thus he could not legally collect rent from her. But she did not stop there. Ruby Vaughn went on to tell the court that Sheehan had extorted money from her several times for immoral purposes: $100 for fighting the brothel abatement law and $25 to help reopen Levy's Alley after having been closed to prostitution a few years before. The most shocking and poignant item was $25 to help pay Detective Captain David Rich's defense. Vaughn claimed that she refused to pay these sums, so Sheehan diverted her rent money for those purposes to bribe local officials. Sheehan dropped his claim, but Ruby Vaughn became the defendant in a bevy of other court cases, many of them lawsuits from creditors but also in criminal matters. Perhaps this was all Sheehan, using the courts to harass the poor girl for ratting on him.

The beginning of 1915 started as a fairly quiet year for the Sheehans, but by the end of September, a series of legal battles would ultimately lead to the undoing of Boise's crime king. Since the city's administrators believed that their own officers were worthless, they brought in detectives from Portland. The Oregon boys, one of whom was a former professional wrestler who went by the name "Strangler Smith," conducted simultaneous raids on three houses of ill repute at 11:30 p.m. on September 26. The Oxford, Gem and Starling were cleared of their occupants, who were then loaded onto the benches of the police court. Doc and Mae Sheehan were among those arrested but were able to pay $400 for their own bonds, as well as $200 for two of the ladies who worked at the Starling. The Sheehans would end up being convicted on the charges of running a disorderly house and selling liquor without a license. They were ordered to pay a total of $300 in fines, but even more troubling was an injunction filed by Mayor Rodgers to close down their place of business for one year under the abatement law.

The abatement case against the Starling Hotel landed in court in October. Sheehan asked for forty-four witnesses to present themselves to give testimony as to the character of the place, but only eight ended up being called. The most interesting witness for the defense was a prostitute named Effie Cummings, known around town as "Babe Kelly." Cummings testified that she did not live at the Starling as a prostitute; she lived there to provide care for Mae Sheehan's sister, who was sick. Her husband testified that he saw nothing disorderly about the Starling and attacked the honesty of one of the detectives, who, he claimed, knew the lawman from Portland. One of the sticking points for the prosecution was a photo, purported to show Mr. and Mrs. Sheehan, engaged in drunken revelry with Mrs. Cummings and another woman. The photo was passed around the courtroom like boys in the schoolyard.

Despite the testimony to the contrary, Judge Davis agreed with the city, shut down the Starling for one year and ordered the furnishings to be sold unless Sheehan could pay a bond in the amount of the furniture's worth. The next day, Doc Sheehan was reportedly injured inside of his shutdown establishment. The *Idaho Statesman* reported that he had fallen down the stairs, possibly after trying to injure himself with a knife, but some would speculate that someone was trying to bump him off. Boise's legal system would eventually take care of that.

In February, Mr. and Mrs. Sheehan's criminal charges of running a bawdy house went before the court. The first jury to hear the evidence ended with a vote of five to seven after two days of deliberations, and the judge declared the jury hung and a second trial date set. The charges would be dropped in June.

Sometime in May, a man named Alaska L. Roberts rushed into the Ada County Sheriff's Office. From his excited utterances, Sheriff Pfost was able to piece together the story of a group of con men who swindled Roberts out of $3,800 of his hard-earned money. Roberts said that he met a man named Dise at a land sale in February. A few days later, Dise invited Roberts on a trip from Roseberry, a Finnish community northwest of Boise where Roberts had a ranch, to Boise to conduct some business and to see the capitol building. While walking up the capitol steps, Dise spotted a pocketbook, seemingly dropped by its owner. Opening it up, they found a letter addressed to "E.P. Morton, care of Bristol Hotel." The letter detailed some inside information on stocks for the Columbia and Nehalem Railroad, a logging track in Oregon. The stock, the letter said, was about to jump from $1.00 per share to $2.25.

The two men decided that it would be best to try to return the pocketbook at the Bristol. Morton, being very grateful for the return of the pocketbook, gave Dise and Roberts the name of a man named Watson in Caldwell who was prepared to sell his stock in the railroad. Roberts handed over his money and was handed back certificates of stock. A few days later, Roberts realized that Dise, Watson and all the others involved in the sale of the stock were nowhere to be found. He took his stock certificates down to the bank, but the teller told Roberts that the certificates were no good, so Roberts went straight to the police. When Sheriff Pfost heard the physical

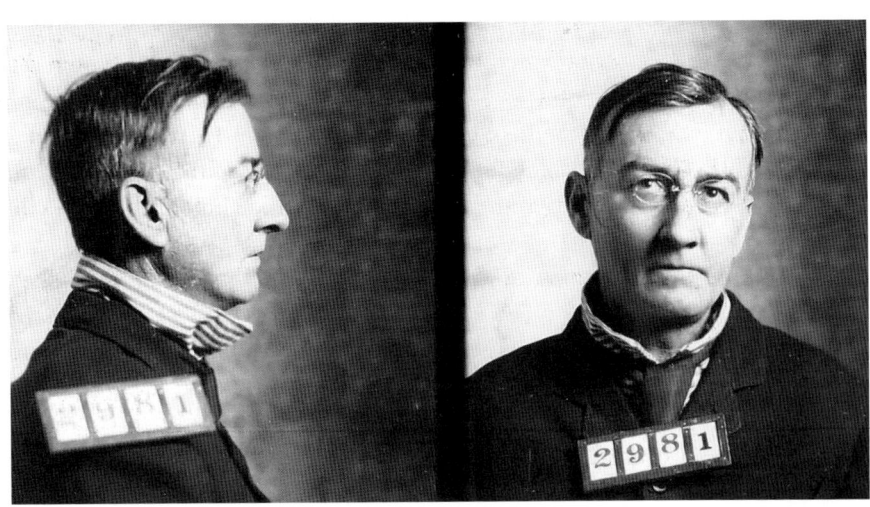

Mugshot of James Adrian "Doc" Sheehan, no. 2981, at the Old Idaho Penitentiary. *Old Penitentiary Prison Records Collection, Idaho State Archives.*

description of the men, he showed Roberts several photographs. The man who called himself Watson was, in fact, James A. "Doc" Sheehan.

Sheriff Pfost arrested Sheehan, charging him with obtaining money by false pretenses. As the lawman tracked down the other conspirators, Sheehan was lodged in the Ada County Jail. It was reported that he was given a whole suite of rooms there, a private bath, a choice of twenty different beds and even a padded cell when he needed quiet time. This probably had less to do with Sheehan's being Boise's Al Capone but because he was the only lodger in the jail at the time. The jail also held two large trunks, which were alleged to belong to Sheehan. The trunks held about twenty-five gallons of liquor.

The trunks were shipped from Salt Lake City in May 1916. When Sheehan was notified that they had arrived in Boise, he went to the Oregon Short Line Railroad station to pick them up. There he found the sheriff waiting for him. Sheehan was arrested, this time charged with transporting liquor through a dry territory, a condition that Idaho had found itself in starting the first day of 1916. During the trial, the trunks of whiskey were brought in, and each juror, as well as the sheriff, was given the opportunity to sample the product, just to make sure that it was, in fact, illegal.

While he was awaiting trial for the bootlegging charge, Sheehan was arrested again and charged with two counts of arson, one stemming from that mysterious fire in Levy's Alley back in 1914 and another for a fire that was set at a private home the same year. Sheehan and another man named Mack Gillum were accused of setting the blazes to defraud the insurance company. One of the primary witnesses in this case was J.J. Oberbilling, a former business partner of Mae Sheehan's. After Oberbilling's testimony, he walked out of the courtroom to find Mae waiting there for him. Before he could react, Mae closed the distance, smacked him in the mouth with her handbag and called him many foul names, leaving off with, "I'll teach you to lie about us." Oberbilling retreated into a side office before she could do any more damage.

Two of the cases pending against Sheehan were finally wrapped up in October. On the second, a jury found him guilty on the transporting liquor charge, and the judge sentenced him to three months in jail with a $150 fine. On the eighteenth, another jury voted to acquit Gillum and Sheehan on the arson charges. The last pending charge against Sheehan could not be resolved so easily. After discussing the matter for twenty-eight hours, the jury in the fraud case could not come to an agreement, voting eight to four with the majority to convict, which was just enough to cause a hung jury. The jurors were sent home, and a new trial date was set for January 1917.

This time there was an agreement, and Sheehan was convicted of obtaining money under false pretenses. The judge ordered Sheehan to serve between one and fourteen years in the penitentiary, and Sheehan's reign as the King of the Tenderloin was over. Ada County's jury pool had to have felt relieved that their workload was about to decrease.

Sheehan's attorney filed appeals in both cases, and Sheehan was allowed to remain free on bond while the courts considered the options. Mae had established the Realty Hotel in the shadow of the Mormon temple in Salt Lake City, but despite it being surrounded by Zion, the Realty did not have a much better reputation than the Starling. Doc was allowed to live there through a special agreement with the court, provided he return when called. When the Idaho Supreme Court struck down both appeals, he lived up to his promise, and on May 6, 1921, Doc Sheehan was admitted to the Idaho State Penitentiary. His hard time would be cut short, though, because eleven months later, he was granted parole based on his poor health. He returned to Mae in Salt Lake City, where he died a few days later of complications from stomach ulcers. In Sheehan's obituary, the Butte, Montana chief of police stated, "I believe he was one of the cleverest of bunco men in the history of crime"—a fitting tribute to the King of the Tenderloin.

Where to See It: Boise's Tenderloin, or red-light district, was in a three-block area that now includes Boise's city hall. So you can say not much has changed there.

THE BUTCHER OF BANNOCK STREET

Henry Neuebaumer was not insane. That was the opinion of cab driver Lee Spangler, who had driven Henry around Boise several times in the days leading up to his violent death behind a billboard at Seventh and Bannock Streets. As the cabman drove his fare about town to take care of various business matters, the two conversed at length, covering various subjects. On two occasions, the two men waited in the cab for up to an hour after they had arrived at Neuebaumer's destination and just talked. Neuebaumer spoke freely, as well as rationally and sanely, but always avoided any personal topics or mention of his troubles. Strangely, during one of these conversations, Henry held across his lap a brand-new double-barrel Ithaca shotgun.

Heinrich Neuebaumer was born in Tuolumne, California, on March 19, 1864. His parents were both immigrants, with his father being born in Germany and his mother in Chile. In 1886, Henry moved from California to Caldwell, where he began an apprenticeship in a blacksmith shop. He earned the reputation around town of being a hard worker. When he was not in the shop, he read books to educate himself in modern business practices. While living in Caldwell, he became acquainted with a rancher named John Powell and began courting his daughter Ms. Ollie Powell. The Powells were well respected, and Ollie was regarded as a perfect lady.

Despite being seventeen years older than Ollie, Henry proved a good candidate for marriage. After learning the blacksmith trade from Al Butts, Henry ended up running the shop. Using the money he earned there, he built his own blacksmith shop. The forge was said to have been a handsome building with plate glass windows, a luxury in the 1890s. In 1897, a group of about a dozen Caldwell men decided to try their luck in the Klondike, but only Henry struck it rich. He had a keen mind made for business and used his earnings from mining to invest in hay and beef speculation in Alaska. It was estimated that by the time of his death, Henry's investments were netting him around $80 per day, upward of $2,300 in 2021 money. He was a well-liked man overall. Once in the Klondike, it was said that he rented out a saloon and paid for everyone's drinks for an entire evening after striking a good claim. He was believed to be a millionaire at the time of his death.

Around 1903, Henry proposed marriage to eighteen-year-old Ollie Powell. Ollie, and most likely her father, accepted. The engagement was mostly long distance because Henry was still very much interested in his business dealings in Alaska. Henry agreed to pay for Ollie to attend college, so in the winter of 1903–4, Ollie enrolled in the Boise Business and Shorthand College, located at Seventh and Main in Boise. The following summer, she gained employment as a clerk with the Idaho Commission Company at its coal office on South Eighth Street. The coal office manager held Ollie in the highest regard, saying that "she was one of the best clerks I have had" and calling her "a perfect little lady." She left employment that October to further her schooling at St. Teresa's Academy, where Henry paid her way. She told Henry that she wanted to study needlework, painting, music and "burnt work" so she could make decorations for when they made their home together. Henry also lavished Ollie with gifts, including gold jewelry, clothing and other incidentals during her time as a student.

The couple decided on a wedding date; they planned to be married on November 12, 1905, at her parents' place in Caldwell. Henry made preparations for managing his businesses in the Klondike and traveled home to Idaho. There, he once again opened his pocketbook to pay for things related to the wedding. Henry gave Ollie $1,200 to buy a trousseau, which usually includes the wedding dress and other clothing and jewelry the bride is to wear on her wedding day. Everything was soon prepared for their nuptials, and Henry was fully expecting to be married to his sweetheart.

Sadly, the day before the wedding was to happen, Henry received the crushing news that Ollie Powell had run off to Boise with a young man named Lafayette Gray. Lafayette had attended the same business school as Ollie, and it is assumed they met there. Gray started visiting Ollie at the Powell home in Caldwell shortly after. Henry was shocked by the news but resolved to do something about it, especially after discovering that Ollie had taken the trousseau and an expensive valise with her. He followed the young couple to the city to retrieve these items, asking around boardinghouses and hotels for them. Henry found that a couple matching their description checked in at the Angus Hotel. In the register was written "J.B. Johnston and Wife, Hagerman."

Incensed further that Ollie and Lafayette were posing as man and wife under a different name, certainly a scandal in 1905, Henry went back to Caldwell and swore out a warrant for grand larceny. Two days after Ollie and Lafayette checked into the Angus, Canyon County deputy sheriff Payne appeared at the front desk. Deputy Payne, with the assistance of Detective Johnson, returned the couple to Canyon County on the westbound train the next morning. The proprietor only learned that the couple had checked in under fake names two days later, when Lafayette sent for the personal property they left behind at the hotel.

Back in Caldwell, Ollie was interviewed by police, promising that she would return all of the property she had taken. Detective Johnson, satisfied with her promise, walked out of the interview room to see Henry and Lafayette having words in the hall. When Lafayette saw the detective, he ran behind Johnson, grabbed him by the shoulders and shouted, "He is going to kill me! Don't let him shoot!" Johnson saw Henry with his hand in his pocket, getting ready to pull out his revolver. The detective seized the gun from Henry but returned it to him the next day. Ollie went before the justice of the peace to answer to the charge of theft.

Henry made it clear how much he had spent on Ollie over the last three years, and like a good businessman, he knew the numbers by heart. Altogether, he had spent $1,240 in cash, $402.50 in jewelry, $152 for clothing and $26 for a silver service, totaling just over $1,800. Henry claimed that she returned about $90 worth of clothing and gave him a promissory note for $105, to be paid in a year's time. She repeated her promise to return everything she could, and Henry withdrew the charge. When Henry asked if Ollie had any money to take care of herself with, she apparently replied that she only had $1 and some chicken feed to her name. Taking pity, Henry gave her $50 to hold her over until she found work, telling her, "Please do not go wrong and sin." After receiving Ollie's promise to pay him back, Henry went to consult with his attorney, former Idaho governor James T. Morrison. Morrison advised his client just to let the matter rest and forget about Ollie Powell. Henry promised that he would do just that and returned to Alaska.

Governor Morrison was somewhat surprised, however, when Henry walked back into his office unannounced on Wednesday, January 17.

Morrison had received a letter from Henry dated December 28 from Alaska, but he had not mentioned any intent to return to Idaho. Henry asked Morrison to transfer all of his Idaho-based properties to his brother. He refused to tell Morrison exactly why he needed this done, and Morrison just assumed that it was the result of some business trouble back in Alaska. He therefore executed the request. Henry also wanted to settle his accounts with Morrison, who had been in charge of collecting money from Henry's business in Idaho. To that end, Morrison drew up a check for $1,419, to be sent to Henry's brother. His business matters taken care of, Henry bid Morrison goodbye and left his office for the last time.

That Friday, a woman rang Morrison's home on the telephone and asked for the governor. He was out, but the caller tried again on Saturday, receiving the same result. The caller then tried Morrison at his office, where he was working that day. The person on the other end of the line turned out to be Ms. Ollie Powell, informing Morrison that Henry had been seen around Boise and asking if the governor knew of the man's whereabouts. He did not know where Henry was but told her that he would try to find out. She called again the next day, and the conversation led Morrison to believe that Ollie and Henry had already met after he returned to Boise. In fact, she had received a note from Henry asking her to meet him at Tenth and Grove that Friday, but she had written back to him refusing the meeting. Ollie, according to those who were with her during this time, seemed unafraid of Henry.

Morrison found out after the fact that Henry was either out making plans for the following Monday morning or in one of two hotel rooms in Boise. When he arrived, he checked himself into the Angus, where he took a page from his rival and signed in under a fake name: "H. Nelson of Portland." He stayed at the Angus from Wednesday when he arrived until Thursday evening around 5:00 p.m., when he took Lee Spangler's cab from the Angus over to the Lauraine, another lodging house. The Lauraine was located at Seventh and Idaho Streets, just one block away from the home of Robert and Ellen Gray, Lafayette's parents. The Grays had a home in Pine, Elmore County, Idaho, but often spent part of the year in Boise. The Grays' Boise home was located at 620 Bannock Street in 1906 in full view of workers constructing the dome of the Idaho capitol building.

When Henry checked into the Angus, he had been accompanied by another man, who signed the register as "J. Maynard, Seattle." The proprietor of the Angus thought that the pair were detectives, as did the landlady of the Lauraine. On Thursday or Friday, Maynard was seen standing in the

Looking south from the Idaho Capitol tower at the rear of the Gray House, second from the left, in 1913. *ID-70-10.406, Idaho State Archives.*

rain on the corner of Seventh and Main, attracting the attention of several people in a barbershop across the street. After a few moments, the barber, Jack Allison, realized that he knew the man. Recognizing Maynard as a fellow Klondike miner, Allison went out to greet him, but while confirming his name to Allison, he declined to come into the shop to talk out of the rain. Maynard said that he was waiting for someone but simply stood on the corner for another hour before walking off alone. He was observed waiting for someone at the same location on another day that week as well.

It was Saturday when Henry called the cab company to request Lee Spangler to come pick him up from the Lauraine. He asked the cabbie to take him over to the Carlson-Lusk Hardware Store at Eighth and Main. In the store, Henry spoke with a clerk named C.M. Bollinger, who reported that Henry had asked him for a good shotgun. Bollinger handed Henry a hammerless smoothbore Ithaca double-barrel with no choke. The weapon was not of the highest quality or expense, yet Henry readily accepted it. He asked Bollinger for shotgun shells, and when the clerk asked how many boxes he wanted, Henry told him, "One box is enough as I only want to use a couple of them." After checking, Bollinger realized that he did not have any shells loaded with buckshot in stock, so he called over to Lorre and Sons hardware to make sure Henry could get the shells there. Henry pulled out a wad of cash to pay for the shotgun and got back in the cab. Spangler drove over to Lorre and Sons, where Henry secured a box of shells filled with no. 5 buckshot. Spangler then drove Henry back to the Lauraine, where, instead of Henry getting out, he struck up a long conversation with the driver. Spangler even got into the backseat to talk to the man while he held the shotgun on his lap. The next day, Sunday, Spangler again drove Henry to a place near Seventh and Jefferson, a block north of Lafayette Gray's parents' home. Again, the two men sat in the cab and conversed for a long time.

On Monday morning, just after 9:00 a.m., Mr. Adna Hall was walking from his home at 316 Bannock Street to work at the First National Bank. Up ahead, he watched a young woman walk out of the house at 620 Bannock. She had a spring in her step, like she was happy and excited. Behind her, a young man stopped to close the door of the house and followed her to the sidewalk. As the young woman, later identified as Ms. Ollie Powell, was passing through the gate, the sound of a shotgun blast rang out from across the street. Ollie fell to the sidewalk, and Lafayette, who had been trying to catch up to her, started running toward his girlfriend but then stopped and turned back toward the house. Ollie managed to stand up and, covered in her own blood, staggered back toward the house by herself. Lafayette bounded up the steps, but as he was about to reach the top step, a second shot rang out and he fell to the ground.

Mr. Hall looked to his left, where he saw a billboard at street level, directly across from the Gray home. Behind the billboard stood a man reloading a double-barrel shotgun. Hall started toward the victims to render aid, but the man behind the billboard motioned for him to step back—advice Hall heeded. The terrified screaming of two women brought Hall's attention back to the front of the house, as Mrs. Ellen Gray, Lafayette's mother, and Ms. Lillian Gray, his little sister, came to the door after hearing the first two shots. Lillian went to Lafayette and tried to help him up, but the third shot from the shotgun struck her arm. Lillian reported later that she did not feel much pain, but her arm went limp and she ran back into the house as she saw her mother drop to her knees in the doorway, apparently injured by buckshot from the same shell that had struck her daughter.

Lafayette began to try to regain his feet, but a fourth shot rang out and again Lafayette went down. The gunman reloaded once more and put the final shotgun shell into his weapon. As Mr. Robert Gray reached the doorway of the home, the fifth shot rang out. Perhaps the adrenaline caught up with Henry or perhaps the encroaching crowd and police officers responding to the scene made him panic, but for some reason the shot missed its mark, except for a single piece of buckshot that tattered the strap on Mr. Gray's suspenders. Having emptied the box of shotgun shells into the Gray family, the shooter pulled his .41-caliber Colt revolver from his pocket and placed it against his right temple. When he pulled the trigger, the shot entered his head, making a ghastly wound, before exiting out the left side of his head

Mr. and Mrs. Gray. *Photo by Karen Lawrence, Ancestry.com.*

and then striking a fence post. Witnesses standing near the billboard reported hearing the crunch of bone as the bullet passed through the man's skull.

Lillian had passed all the way through the house and walked out of the backdoor, where she found a man walking through the alley. She begged for help, but the man was confused. He asked if the person who had shot her was still in the house, a question she could not answer because the location of the shooter was not apparent to the victims. The man, H.C. Myer, tried to convince Lillian to go to the Sherman Boarding House with him, but she cried out that she had to go back to the front of the house because her mother and brother had also been shot. Myer went around to the front of the house, where a crowd was gathering around Lafayette, who was begging them not to let him be shot again. Someone asked who had shot him, and Lafayette replied, "Henry Neuebaumer."

As Boise police officers surrounded and guarded Henry's body, ambulances arrived to take the wounded to the hospitals, Ollie and Lafayette to St. Lukes

Boise Street Railroad, trackage on Bannock Street looking east between Seventh and Eighth Streets. The passenger depot is visible at right. *ID-75-65-32, Idaho State Archives.*

and Lillian and her mother to St. Alphonsus. Lillian had been struck twice, once in her right side and again on the other in the fleshy part of her right forearm. Mrs. Ellen Gray had a pretty serious wound through her abdomen that was expected to kill her. The outlook proved similarly grim for the young lovers. Lafayette had six pieces of shot lodged inside his body. His right arm was shattered and he had a wound over his temple, but the most serious wound was in his abdomen. Doctors were not sure that he could survive.

However, Ollie had been injured the worst. The doctor who attended to her told the *Statesman* that she was "literally shot to pieces." Three shots shattered her arm, and three more entered her legs. One went into her stomach, and one went through her right lung, a wound the doctor said she could not possibly survive. Ollie's family, including her parents and two sisters with their husbands, gathered around her hospital bed after she left surgery. In pain and agony, Ollie lingered and was able to speak in intervals to her parents. She expressed no ill feelings toward the man whose jealous rage caused her fatal injuries. On Tuesday, at 3:14 a.m., Ollie's suffering ended. She was taken to Caldwell, where she was buried at Canyon Hill Cemetery the next day. Her parents chose not to mark Ollie's grave, and it remains unmarked to this day.

As police investigated the scene, they found that Henry had concealed himself behind the billboard for some time, waiting to spring his murderous

Left: Lafayette Gray on his wedding day. *Karen Lawrence, via Ancestry.*

Below: Ollie Powell's unmarked grave at Canyon Hill Cemetery in Caldwell. *IdaHistory Collection.*

trap on Ollie and Lafayette. There was some straw on the ground that looked as if a man had been lying down on it. He was also found with two overcoats, enough to keep him comfortable out in the chilly January weather in Boise. Inside his pockets were found several letters written to different people, mostly explaining his actions and making final arrangements. One letter was to the *Idaho Statesman*. The letter was soon after reprinted in the paper in its entirety. After a brief explanation of what he felt was Ollie's treachery toward him, Henry said, "[A]nd now I shall learn her a lesson which will be her just dues. She cannot make a fool of me again."

The letter to the sheriff and coroner asked that Henry's brother Edouard be notified of the crime. When Edouard received notification, he immediately boarded a train from California. Upon his arrival in Boise, Edouard was given the letter his now late brother had written. Henry left a tantalizing bit of information in the letter by informing Edouard that he had buried quite a bit of gold dust on the Yukon River. The gold, Henry said, was hidden just in case "there is another life, and I ever come back to this world." Since he hid it for his own future self to find, he did not reveal the location, even to his brother, to whom he left the rest of his fortune. Thus, it may be possible that a cache of gold dust belonging to the Butcher of Bannock Street sits somewhere along an Alaskan river, waiting to be found—if it has not been retrieved by its owner from a previous life.

WHERE TO SEE IT: Ollie Powell was buried at Canyon Hill Cemetery in Caldwell in an unmarked grave. The Gray home at 620 Bannock Street was later bulldozed to make room for Capitol Park, now known as Governor Clint Andrus Park. The location of the billboard behind which Henry Neumbaumer shot Ollie Powell and the Gray family is now the AT&T building at 629 West Bannock Street.

THE WARM PLUNGE OF DEATH

For about four and a half decades, Boise's famous natatorium was a popular pleasure destination for Boiseans and tourists alike. The "Nat," as it came to be called, was developed by German-born and trained architect John C. Paulsen, who also designed a similar structure in Helena, Montana, named the Broadwater Natatorium. Long before Europeans stepped foot in the Boise Valley, the native Shoshone utilized the hot springs along the Boise River for a number of purposes. Soon after the founding of Boise City, settlers realized the value of the geothermal energy lying below their feet. What is now the oldest and largest geothermal system in the country is currently used to heat several homes and government buildings in Boise.

Despite all of the good times and pleasant memories made at the Nat, dark and tragic ones also came to pass. The first death in the natatorium's pool occurred the very first day water from the geothermal well filled the space, on March 31, 1892. The previous day, the Nat's superintendent issued an order that everyone not working on the building was to keep out, but that did not stop Frank Dymond from sneaking in for a swim. Dymond's friend C.C. Gallintine, a carpenter working at the Nat, had invited Dymond to go swimming. The night watchman also knew Gallintine, so the two were granted access to the building.

After the two men disrobed and entered the warm water, Gallintine asked Dymond if he could swim. Dymond said he could not, so Gallintine warned him to stay in the shallow end, but soon Dymond moved beyond the safety line to deeper water and began to struggle. Gallintine tried to grab the drowning

Natatorium exterior. *Postcard by Wesley Andrews Inc., 1920.*

Natatorium swimming pool, Boise. *ID-1981-A, Idaho State Archives.*

Natatorium streetcar. *Hugh Hartman Collection.*

man and pull him to safety, but he was not a strong swimmer himself and felt his friend's grip start to relax. Dymond yelled, "I'm drowning!" before sinking into the depth of the Plunge. Gallintine went for help, but it would be an hour before the victim's body was recovered.

Dymond's nude body was placed on one of the new electric streetcars built to service the natatorium and carried to the morgue. Dymond was unmarried, so a telegraph was sent to his father in Canada. The coroner empaneled an inquest to determine if Boise Artesian Hot and Cold Water Company was responsible for Dymond's death. Surprisingly, one of the names listed on the coroner's jury is Hosea Eastman, who happened to be the general manager of the Boise Artesian Hot and Cold Water Company. Not surprisingly, the inquest determined that the company was not responsible for the death of Frank Dymond, which turns out to be a common conclusion to each drowning at the Nat.

It was not just the working class that enjoyed, and succumbed to, the deep and dangerously relaxing warm waters of the natatorium. On February 7, 1908, a man seen enjoying a casual swim by a pair of tourists who noticed his apparent skill as a swimmer also fell victim of the geothermal pool. If the pair had been from Boise, they might have recognized William Dudley Field, whose name appeared frequently in the *Idaho Statesman* as having closed many large real estate deals around town. He had been making investments in other cities too, including bayfront property in Astoria,

Oregon. Throughout the first half of 1907, he was traveling extensively to places such as Pendleton, Portland, Spokane and Seattle, looking for new investment opportunities.

It was on one of these trips that Field experienced a strange and sad event. He left Boise in mid-July 1907, en route to Portland, and from there he went to Northern California. He stopped by the Humboldt County Bank, where he deposited $1,000 and asked to be put in contact with an established real estate firm. He returned to the bank later the same day to withdraw some of the cash he had just deposited and followed this by treating several unknown people to a day at the skating rink. There, he seemed like he was having little trouble being parted from his money, handing out large tips and even giving away his gold watch.

The following day, his behavior became erratic when he walked into a cigar store in Arcata, California, and started looking at pipes. Field allegedly took a pipe and walked out of the store without paying for it. He walked up to a random person on the street and gave him the pipe, and he gave the pipe's case to another man. He then walked into another cigar store, grabbed a handful of cigars and once again walked out without paying. Next he entered a saloon, ordered a beer and then threw it away. He was next spotted on the street, a riding whip in hand, standing in the streetcar tracks, forcing the motorman to stop for him. He jumped onto the car, found a seat between two ladies and was apprehended by police when he next got off. Two days later, probably while still in custody, he attempted to hang himself with his own necktie.

Since Field was a member of the Benevolent and Protective Order of the Elks, the local Elks Lodge took responsibility for his care. The Elks were able to contact Mrs. Field, who met her husband in Portland, where he was placed in a hospital to treat a nervous breakdown, a condition he was not initially expected to survive. By September 8, however, he was reported to be "nearly well." Mr. and Mrs. Field returned to Boise a month later; he was back doing business a few days later.

By February, Field could be seen at the natatorium once or twice a week indulging in a swim, probably as treatment for his nervous mental state. The two tourists watched him skillfully swim for a moment before Field exited the pool and went into one of the rooms off to the side of the building. The tourists thought he was leaving for the day, but a few minutes later, Field returned and dove into the Plunge at the far end, where the pool was twelve feet deep. Five or ten minutes later, the spectators noticed that Field had ceased his splashing, and the alarm was raised.

Natatorium from the river side (rear) of the building. *Idaho State Archives.*

One of the attendants, Louis Elopoles, started searching from the poolside and spotted Field on the bottom of the deep end, facedown with his head resting on one of his arms. Without hesitation, Elopoles stripped off his clothes and dove into the pool to attempt a rescue. He was able to pull Field's body to the surface, and other attendants, including the Nat's manager, helped haul his lifeless form to the poolside, where resuscitation efforts began. Two doctors soon arrived and pronounced Field dead. The coroner was then summoned. An investigation of the body found that one of Field's feet was dislocated, leading the coroner to theorize that his foot had struck one of the barrels in the pool indicating the water's depth as he dove into the Plunge. The pain must have shocked him greatly, causing him to lose consciousness.

Mrs. Field was notified of her husband's death by telephone at their residence in the Friedline Apartments, located at 1320 State Street. The Boise Elks took charge of their lodge member's funeral arrangements, and the service was held in the Fields' apartment. Many friends gathered to honor the man and witness his burial at Morris Hill Cemetery. Along with Frank Dymond, he was one of at least nine people to die in the Plunge.

WHERE TO SEE IT: The beautiful, cathedralesque natatorium building was destroyed in a windstorm in 1935, but the pool is still in use by the City of Boise Parks and Recreation Department. Although the pool retained the name of natatorium, there is no grand structure surrounding the deep waters; the Nat is now an outdoor summer recreational attraction. It is located at 1811 East Warm Springs Avenue, behind Adams Elementary.

HOW NOT TO CLEAN A STOVE

Often, the simplest answer to questions of how individuals from the past involved themselves in so many seemingly thickheaded practices is that they knew no better or that they lived in different times and places. Such is the case of twenty-three-year-old Maud Ellen Stone and what occurred on Saturday, September 16, 1905. Having recently extinguished the kitchen stove and believing that the fire within had died, young Maud began to clean the sturdy appliance with a mixture of gasoline and turpentine in the kitchen of her home at 827 East Bannock Street in East Boise. While she scrubbed the surface of the heavy iron stove, a remaining hot ember ignited the hazardous mixture and set a stunned Maud's clothes alight. Reacting fast, she grabbed a blanket and attempted to douse the spreading flames, but the blanket proved too small to be effective and Maud ran from the house in panic. Luckily, the Stones' home sat beside a small irrigation canal, into which the severely burned Maud flung herself, turning over to extinguish any remaining flames. With horrible burns about her throat and arms, Maud was taken inside her home, and a physician hastened to the Stone residence, where the doctor determined that her wounds were not life-threatening. However, as a Christian Scientist, she would not accept much-needed medical treatment. As her wounds became infected, Maud's health began to falter. She died of her injuries at 1:30 a.m. on October 5, 1905, after lingering for three weeks in what must have been excruciating pain. Two and a half weeks later, on October 24, 1905, the *Idaho Daily Statesman* ran an ad listing the property as "For Sale—At a Bargain, a 6-room house finely furnished, electric lights, city water, closets, woodshed, lot 50x132, fenced." It seems that the pain of losing his wife in such a terrible manner induced W.G. Stone to flee the scene of such tragedy.

WHERE TO SEE IT: Maud now rests at Morris Hill Cemetery, Section C, Block 31, Plot 4. The parcel on which she passed away, 827 East Bannock Street, no longer exists; it was added to another lot to form another, larger property.

AN OLD PIONEER MEETS A MODERN DEATH

When Charles Villenueve first started mining in the Boise Basin in 1863, he probably had no idea what technological wonders he would see during his lifetime. After the Boise Basin gold rush slowed and the claims stopped paying out as much, Charles took his earnings and moved to the Boise Valley, where he homesteaded 140 acres near Star. In 1872, he married Martha Anderson and used his experience as a stonecutter to build a home out of Boise River rock in 1881. Five years later, the Villenueves sold their home, now in the National Register of Historic Places, and moved to Boise City, then in the midst of a great period of modernization. By 1887, the first electric light had been turned on during the town's Fourth of July celebration, an event that led to the creation of an electric railway system with service commencing in 1891. From the original streetcar line running down Warm Springs Avenue, the Boise Interurban would develop, eventually connecting Boise to Caldwell, with service to many communities in between. The Boise Valley Loop, as the route would be referred to, provided the transportation needs of businessmen, freight interests and pleasure seekers, as well as an expedient link to the direct Union Pacific line in Nampa, Idaho. A person could take a dip in the Plunge at the natatorium in the morning, stop at Pierce Park for lunch and go fishing at Lake Lowell in the afternoon, all while having to rely on just the Interurban to get around.

On the evening of March 11, 1910, Charles Villenueve had finished some masonry work at the home of Mrs. Stella Grebst in the Greenwood Precinct near Eagle and was returning home to Boise on the Interurban car, due to

Above: Charles Villenueve family. *From left to right*: Martha, Fred, Mary, Godfrey (Charles), Theresa and Nicholas. *ID-P19866.0026.0004, Idaho State Archives.*

Opposite, top: Charles Villenueve House outside Eagle, Idaho, built in 1881. *IdaHistory Collection.*

Opposite, bottom: Looking down the main street of Eagle as the Interurban travels west, circa 1907. *ID-2010.M.18, Eagle Museum of History and Preservation.*

arrive in the city at 7:15 p.m. When the car in which he was riding reached the intersection of Edgewood Road and Valley Road, today's Highway 44, just around three-fourths of a mile west of Pierce Park, he realized that he had forgotten his overcoat. He told Mr. R.D. Webb, who lived at the ranch, that he needed to go back for it, and Charles exited the car with Webb. Webb went home assuming that Charles would catch the next car going west. As Webb settled into bed, he heard the approaching car and remarked to his wife that Charles was probably catching it so he could retrieve his overcoat. However, instead of the normal sound of an interurban car arriving at the station, Webb heard the shrillness of an emergency whistle and the squeal of brakes grinding against the tracks.

The scene outside was horrifying. Charles Villeneuve lay dead on the track, his skull caved in and both legs broken. The front of the trolley was damaged. The streetcar motorman told the coroner's jury that he saw the man too late, approximately when the car was a short 150 feet away. Charles just stood there, one foot over the track and waving at the driver as if he were trying to flag down the car. Despite several warning whistles and the

noise from the brakes, Charles stood in place until the car struck him. After contact, the car traveled another 80 feet before coming to a rest. Employees of the Interurban loaded Charles's body on the Boise-bound car and took him to the funeral home of Schreiber and Sidenfaden, where Coroner Schreiber instantly recognized the body. To make certain, he went to the Villeneuve home at 622 Hayes Street. There, he verified that Charles had not returned home. Charles's son Nick accompanied the coroner back to the funeral home and made positive identification of the body.

A coroner's inquest was arranged, and the jury was asked to determine whether fault rested with the Interurban Company or the old pioneer. After weighing the evidence presented, the six men returned a verdict that Interurban was "not responsible," adding that there was no way the company could have avoided the tragedy. Nick Villeneuve speculated that the headlights on the car contributed to his father's death; the glare led to Charles's inability to properly judge the speed or distance of the car coming toward him. Charles was buried in the St. John's section of Morris Hill Cemetery, an Idaho pioneer who fell victim to changing technology. The Interurban met the same fate in 1928, when automobiles became more efficient and reliable enough to move people around the valley.

Where to See It: Charles is buried in Section SJ3, Block 4, Space 5 at Morris Hill Cemetery. The site of the accident took place at the approximate intersection of Edgewood Lane and Old State Street in west Eagle, Idaho. Most of the infrastructure making up the Interurban was torn out, but evidence can still be seen around the valley, including "The Hat," which is now a bus stop in front of the College of Idaho in Caldwell.

A DARK DAY IN THE CAPITOL OF LIGHT

Elevator operator Oscar Kelly and janitor Frank Rhienhart were two of the few people working in Idaho's state capitol building on December 18, 1926. It was the Saturday before Christmas, the offices were empty and few visitors roamed the People's House to see where state laws are made and to check out the exhibits showcasing Idaho's history and ways of life. Around 12:45 p.m., the two men heard a *thud* followed by a crash coming from the mineral exhibit on the first floor. They rushed to the scene, where they found injured nine-year-old Grant Ward. They began to bandage the child's head as Dr. Alfred Budge was sent for. When the doctor arrived, he determined that they needed to get the boy to the hospital right away, but little Grant died en route to St. Alphonsus. The entire top of Grant's skull was crushed, and his left wrist was broken.

When the police and coroner examined the scene, they quickly determined that Grant had fallen into the mineral exhibit from above. Due to a lack of witnesses, the police resorted to educated guesswork to draw some conclusions about what may have caused the boy to fall. Grant had been working as a magazine carrier and had just dropped off some magazines at the courthouse before climbing the marble stairs inside the capitol. He went all the way up to the offices on the fourth floor, dropped off some papers and then headed back down. Except, it seems that he decided to slide down the balustrade from the fourth to the third floor to save some time or to break up the monotony of magazine deliveries. Where the rail makes a nearly ninety-degree turn, he lost his balance, tried unsuccessfully to gain a handhold on

Idaho Capitol staircase, circa 1913. *IdaHistory Collection.*

the marble and fell. On the way down, Grant hit the railing on the second floor, which deflected his body down to the first floor and into the mineral exhibit, where his head struck one of the ore samples.

For most of the people who examined the scene, a tragic accident seemed to be the logical conclusion, and no one seemed to think that foul play was involved despite the lack of witnesses. The coroner, however, considered calling an inquest to examine the facts. He speculated that a coroner's jury could perhaps present recommendations to prevent a similar action from happening in the future. Ultimately, due mostly to cost, an inquest was never held. Additionally, no changes to make the capitol building's balustrades more secure were made. The building caretakers stressed that this was the first such accident in the capitol since that section was completed in 1912. Ultimately, blame rested with the boy and his youthful sense of recklessness. John Craig, custodian of the building, said, "Children have always been our main problem, and remain even more of a problem."

Two days later, Iva and Clarence Ward buried their child at the Morris Hill Cemetery. The funeral was packed with mourners, and Grant's friends served as pallbearers. Grant's parents struggled with grief over the loss of their child. Family members reported that Clarence would not allow Christmas carols to be played in the family homes after Grant died. Visitors to the capitol still ask about where the boy died and point to the red stains on the marble floors as evidence of bloodstains, although the red color is actually rust from the iron embedded in the marble floors. Grant's niece worked in the attorney general's office and kept a photograph along with news articles about Grant in her office to help tell the story of a life cut short at such a young age.

WHERE TO SEE IT: Although the mineral exhibit is long gone, visitors to the Idaho state capitol can still climb the steps to the fourth floor and imagine what it would be like to slide down the wide, flat balustrade, although the authors and publishers of this work do not recommend or endorse any attempts at such.

GOING UP—ALL THE WAY TO HEAVEN

The McCarty Building, once owned by businesswoman Martha McCarty and standing proudly on the northeast corner of Ninth and Idaho Streets, opened for business in 1909. While the bottom floor of the building housed the Ballou-Latimer Drug Company, it also possessed an elevator, a notable feature in Boise in those days. Early elevators lacked the safety features of today's models, yet issues did not always arise from the lifts themselves, but rather with their operators and riders. On Tuesday, November 13, 1917, twenty-one-year-old Dora Weise, an employee of the Western Union Telegraph Company, held misgivings about riding the building's lift, especially as the elevator doors began to close. As the operator, in this case a teenage boy, pulled the lever to close the doors, Dora quickly stepped from the elevator; the door struck her hard in the head, causing her to fall back and clutch "the side of the elevator, her feet dangling beneath the car." When the operator stopped the lift, Dora fell into the shaft underneath, breaking her leg and further injuring her head. The manager of the McCarty Building took her to St. Luke's Hospital, where she died several days later on November 17, 1917, at 3:45 p.m. having never regained consciousness.

Not all elevator accidents proved fatal, but most were grisly affairs. When Joseph Sewell attempted to jump onto an already rising freight elevator at the Boise National Bank Building, on the southwest corner of the intersection at Eighth and Idaho in July 1909, he found himself in a nearly "head bursting" predicament. Perhaps he sought to save time or simply wanted to play around, but when Joseph started the elevator, ran to the moving lift and attempted to jump aboard, he must have soon realized that his hasty decision might be his last. None of Joseph's fellow employees witnessed the crisis, but the stricken man's head became caught between the elevator and the floor above, increasing the pressure applied as the machine ascended. Had one Clarence Mitchell not been waiting at the top of the elevator shaft above, Joseph's skull "would have been crushed like an eggshell." Clarence, who was waiting for Joseph to deliver some goods to the top of the building, promptly turned off the machine from above and in the process saved the young man from quite literally losing his head. Surgeons at St. Alphonsus Hospital feared that the damage was done to the injured man's spine and not the wounds inflicted on his head. They did not believe that Joseph would survive the night. However, by August 2, 1909, the *Idaho Daily Statesman* wrote that Joseph Sewell's condition was improving, although he remained paralyzed. However, the 1910 federal census lists Joseph as living with his father, Joseph Sewell Sr., and working as a night watchman in the express or freight industry—a job requiring mobility to perform.

The advancement of elevator technology in future decades did not stop tragedies from occurring, and with regularity. The elevator within the Sonna Building, at the intersection of Ninth and West Main, became a nightmare for Boise patrolman Harry Briggs on Monday, February 20, 1922, when he, like those before, was maimed by a mechanical lift. As Harry recalled, having lived through the accident, while he rode the elevator, the power went out, causing the engine to stop running and the lift to become stuck. The elevator car had frozen in place only several inches below the floor on its route down the shaft, a scenario that gave Harry a false sense of security, for he began to step from the elevator when the car began to fall, striking the patrolman's head in the process and causing internal injuries to the kidneys as well.

Witnesses, however, were on the scene and told a different set of events in which Harry acted hastily by failing to heed the sensible advice of those around him: janitor F.W. Engelke, elevator operator Speed Garrett and two other riders. According to these witnesses, the elevator stalled three feet below floor level when the power went out. At this point, stated Engelke, "the patrolman became excited and demanded that he be let out at once." Speed Garrett provided a stool kept in the elevator and positioned it under the door. At this point, the two men claimed, a panicked Harry jumped up with so much force he knocked himself nearly unconscious and fell backward into the elevator car. Engelke informed *Idaho Daily Statesman* reporters that when the power goes out, the elevators do not budge and

The Old Elks Building at the corner of Ninth and Jefferson, Boise, Idaho. *IdaHistory Collection.*

that locking mechanisms can only be disengaged when the power is once again turned on. Either Harry hit his head so hard that he forgot exactly what happened or the injured man was attempting to maintain his dignity by blurring the truth. Yet the fact remains that it is smart practice to never try and abandon a stuck elevator.

A short two years later at the Elks Building, sitting on the southeast corner of Ninth and Jefferson, two workmen, Frank Litche and H.V. Kohler, survived a brush with death despite the exceedingly severe injuries they sustained when a fellow worker failed to use common sense, starting the elevator while the two men worked atop the elevator. As the elevator began to travel upward, the men became trapped between the shaft's wall and the car; as they began to scream in pain and terror, the workman responsible for the accident cut the power, stopping the elevator. Frank Litche suffered a broken pelvis, five broken ribs and multiple lacerations about the head. H.V. Kohler's skull was fractured, and his face showed multiple lacerations. The lift had only traveled four feet, had the elevator car not been stopped then, the *Idaho Daily Statesman* reported, the two men would have been crushed to death. Despite their serious injuries, both men survived.

On December 14, 1947, seven-year-old Nancy Thunemann entered the elevator at the Mode Department Store, on Eighth and Idaho Streets, when her leg somehow slipped between the door and the floor of the department store. Nancy began to scream, alerting her mother to her plight. When firefighters arrived, Nancy helped them as they cut away

Top: The Mode on Eighth Street, Boise, Idaho. *IdaHistory Collection*.

Bottom: Morler's Cyclery Shop. *ID-1970-140-001, Idaho State Archives*.

portions of the elevator car to free her twisted and broken leg from the door. Happily, Nancy survived her injuries and kept her injured limb as well. Yet, as late as 1952, Boise experienced fatal elevator accidents. Sixty-five-year-old Albert Call was killed by a falling service elevator car at the Morler Cyclery Shop at 415 North Tenth Street. Although the car dropped only ten feet when the hoist broke, the damage done to the car was enough to kill Albert. Elevators would improve over the following decades, fitted with better cables and much improved braking systems, but as for us, we'll take the escalator.

WHERE TO SEE IT: The McCarty Building still sits at the northeast corner of Ninth and Idaho, with the building's lobby and elevator easily accessible to the public. The Boise National Bank Building is located on Eighth and Idaho; it houses several popular restaurants as well as a historic bank vault in the basement. The Sonna Building is still on the northwest corner of Ninth and Main, while the Mode Department Store Building, now a cocktail bar selling delicious adult beverages, rests on the northwest corner of Eighth and Idaho. Dora Weise is interred at Morris Hill Cemetery in Boise, Section St. John's 4, Block 30, Lot 8. Albert Call can be found at Cloverdale Memorial Park at Fairview Avenue and Cloverdale Road in west Boise.

FAILURE TO RAISE THE DEAD

The Strange Afterlife of Boise's Edith Peshak

Under the well-manicured lawn of Boise's historic Morris Hill Cemetery rests whatever remains of Edith Peshak, a Boise citizen with a particularly interesting and macabre afterlife. Riddled with cancer and desperate to find a cure, Edith and her husband, Elmer, moved to the Home of Truth, a religious commune in the deserts of southeastern Utah's San Juan County, in April 1934. The community they joined was devoted to the post-apocalyptic teachings of its founder, a wealthy New Jersey widow and aspiring spiritualist named Marie Ogden, who came to the deserts of Utah with her original followers in September 1933. Ogden had recruited most of her early followers from Idaho's capital city the year before. In an interview with freelance journalist Hector Lee, given on March 5, 1946, Marie informed Lee that "in 1933, at the beginning of the year, I made a trip to the West, coming as far as Chicago, and then on to Boise, Idaho, to meet people who were then reading some of the material I was writing, and who were interested in the idea of promoting a colony or settlement where people who were of our thought and mind could…develop a place to live and begin life anew, so to speak." She eventually recruited twenty-one followers from Boise, relocating them to the concentric confines of her desert commune, to Marie—a modern-day Noah's Ark.

Before she came to Boise in 1933, Marie was a woman of means who, following the death of her husband, Isaac Harry Ogden, in 1929, inherited his fortune and, with it, power she never experienced while he still lived. Marie Margaret Matilda Schneider was born in Newark, New Jersey,

Above: Grave of Edith Peshak at Morris Hill Cemetery, Boise, Idaho. *IdaHistory Collection.*

Right: Marie Ogden. *ID-5057.2 Monticello Museum Collection, San Juan Historical Commission.*

Opposite: San Juan County, Home of Truth *No. 917.92-10797, Utah State Historical Society.*

in 1883, where she came of age. At nineteen years old, Marie Schneider became Marie Ogden after she married Harry, then a successful executive at a regional insurance company. By twenty, she was pregnant with a daughter, giving birth to Roberta Ogden in April 1904. Her marriage to Harry seems to have been a loving one, as she spoke of him in interviews given later in life with a sense of loss and grief. Additionally, she certainly lived the busy life of a socialite, joining various associations, clubs, charitable foundations and welfare societies, yet in her writings she describes her boredom with life, stating, "All days alike—terrible monotony of daily trips with unhappy outlook ahead." Like many, Marie longed for a deeper meaning to her life. After Harry's death, Marie continued to live the lifestyle of a well-to-do urbanite, but like many women of her day and age, she also approached Spiritualism as an intellectual pursuit to take up her time and make life interesting, but also as a way to attempt to communicate with dead loved ones. Marie's study of Spiritualism eventually sparked the creative process that would later develop into her guiding ideology, the belief system that would outline her mortal and spiritual existence and those of her followers.

At this transitional period in her life, Marie created her new theology by drawing from "astrology, divination and biblical scripture." She has been quoted as saying that her "theosophy integrates strands of Christian devotion and recondite practices." Consequently, in 1929, she met William Dudley Pelley, a former journalist of foreign affairs, a failed screenplay writer and self-fashioned spiritual demagogue. He rose to prominence in the United States in the 1920s after he purported to have died in a hotel room in Altadena, California. Pelley described the sensation of falling through the floor and waking outside of the earthly realm in a large blue space. His "experience" was printed in national magazines, the first publication being *American* magazine. He said that heavenly beings gave him instructions pertaining to maintaining the segregation of the "races," rules he wrote down in a book about racial differences. The title of Pelly's book was *Seven Minutes to Eternity*, a report in which he asserted of the races, "They're the great classifications of humanity epitomizing gradations of spiritual development, starting with the black man and proceeding upward in cycles to the white." He also involved himself in the study of the occult. Through this medium, he and Marie began conversing. They both shared an apocalyptic worldview fashioned into the ideologies on which they would establish their respective religious and social movements.

Through Pelley, Marie was introduced to the channeling of the divine through a vessel, or an "oracle," as Pelley referred to his spiritual muses, from whence he claimed to have received the content for his *Liberation Scripts*. When Adolf Hitler began his rise to power, especially after 1929, Pelley began to support Hitler's racist and authoritarian tactics—even creating a white nationalist group based on the Nazi SA known as the Silver Legion. Marie cut ties with her counterpart. As Pelley spread words of hate that targeted America's Jewish population, Marie's views, that the end was indeed coming, only became stronger given her observation of Pelley and Hitler's coming to power. After cutting ties with Pelley, Marie maintained that she, too, could speak to God. In 1929, Marie began to teach her early followers about her apocalyptic revelations in Newark, New Jersey. She started the process of recruiting followers to her school, the School of Truth, a group she had established in 1930, to join her in founding the Home of Truth in the dry wilderness of southeastern Utah.

As the leader of the School of Truth, Marie claimed to be an oracle, an individual chosen to receive messages from God and God's emissaries. She received a vision while in New York, in which she "dreamed a dream, and in that dream, she saw a valley, and above the valley, the word 'Utah,' a chronicle similar to that of her Mormon neighbors. Ogden 'knew instantly,' she later recalled, 'it was the place.'" Believing that she had received instruction from the creator, Marie packed up a car and hit the road in 1933, traveling first to Chicago and then on to Boise in 1933. She had been in contact with the Peshak family in Boise since 1931 or 1932; the family had impressed the Spiritualist. Of the Peshaks, Marie would say, "It was pleasant to realize that a family living on the outskirts of a large city were so interested in the

San Juan County, Home of Truth. *No. 917.92-10796, Utah State Historical Society.*

deeper things of life, and in such manner indicated that they might become members of the Community." It came to pass that when Marie found out about Edith Peshak's cancer after one of her lectures, she began trying to convince Edith that a cure existed within the tenets of her teachings. Edith, in turn, came to believe that Marie communicated directly with God because she informed her followers that she received divine revelations through the medium of her typewriter. One message she received tasked her with establishing a community in the deserts of San Juan County, just outside Monticello, Utah. Another revelation instructed her how to cure individuals racked with illness and hovering at death's door. This is why, in April 1934, the desperate Peshaks moved to a commune in the dry and barren deserts of San Juan County, Utah.

Marie believed as the divine messenger foretold, that the location where the Home of Truth was founded would become a refuge to those few chosen to survive the end of days. In this sanctuary, Marie and her followers constructed buildings of wood and stone within three concentric circles—the outer, middle and the inner portals. Ogden claimed the inner

Marie Ogden at her typewriter. *ID-20230, Monticello Museum Collection, San Juan Historical Commission.*

portal as her home and declared that it was the exact center of Earth's axis. These circles, she informed her followers, would be the last livable space for humanity after Armageddon—an "ark" on which humanity would be saved. The members of the community worked tirelessly to erect crude homes, a house of worship, an assembly hall and other necessary structures. They also grew their own crops, refrained from eating meat except for fish, abstained from alcohol, did not smoke, steered clear of coffee and gave up all their worldly possessions. Edith and Elmer accepted these terms, and following her arrival at the retreat, a deathly ill Edith placed her faith completely in Marie's self-proclaimed abilities, including her capacity to heal the sick and resurrect the dead. To her credit, Marie tried to save the stricken woman, despite her expectations being totally impossible for Edith to fulfill. Edith, the "healer" asserted, could cure herself if she ignored her pain and focused on her faith as well as in her ability to cure herself of the negative thoughts that had turned into matter—the sickness within. Any failure in the "treatment" was interpreted as being due to Peshak's lack of faith. The daily "treatment" included the laying of hands, prayer, song and the application of oils. However, Edith died of cancer on February 11, 1934, at the age of fifty. Marie refused to pronounce Edith dead, instead telling her followers that she rested between worlds.

Over the next four months, Edith's body was ritually bathed in salt solutions, given egg and milk enemas and blessed with the hands of her friends and family on her. The process of reincarnation turned out to be rather grim, and many of her one hundred followers left the commune. Yet Marie insisted that her rituals were all part of the resurrection process. Marie asserted that she was communicating with Edith on a daily basis, as well as receiving instruction from what she referred to as "unseen friends," or beings from the other side. The voices instructed Marie to bathe the "outer form" on a daily basis, change the bed linens daily due to the mess caused by "rectal feeding" and to do anything else required to "cleanse the lower organism." Despite all the attention, Marie felt that her "patient" was losing ground, although she was heartened when "there were decided manifestations of Life Within the Body…these included discharge of blood from the nostrils, and from the lower organism, and also other natural discharge of waste matter." Marie declared that only she could feel the pulse "vibrations" Edith was displaying because only she had the sixth sense to discern them. After a few months, the corpse's skin "took on a parchment-like appearance and feel, and the flesh began to shrink around its extremities." As Edith's body deteriorated, Marie informed her remaining followers that their patient's body was "dematerializing," while the "astral form" was being born anew in another body. Doubt, assuredly, lingered within the minds of Marie's remaining followers.

Ultimately, while Edith's remains were successfully mummified, her resurrection was a failure. Edith was well on her way to mummification when her daughter Helen contacted San Juan county attorney Donald Adams to voice her concerns about her mother's remains. Her mother's corpse had, in fact, been reposing in a cabin in the Outer Portal, being slowly dehydrated by the hot, dry air of southeast Utah. Adams went and paid a visit to the Home of Truth, trying to find out the facts about Edith's remains. When he approached Marie, she told him that Edith still lived and was only in a state between both the living and the dead, that the cord connecting the two had not been severed. Edith, Marie informed Adams, must choose which world she wanted to live in. She had not yet decided. Marie would not let Adams view the body, and he went away without visual confirmation. She refused Adams entry once again when he returned with the sheriff. She did agree to grant access to Edith to Dr. I.W. Allen and a nurse when the authorities returned to the colony. When Allen made the journey to the settlement

Mrs. Peshak's body, illustration, from the *Omaha Evening Bee-News*, December 29, 1935. *ID-sn95073287, Library of Congress.*

with nurses Leda Young and Dorothy Bayles, Young recalled that Marie blocked their way as they approached via the road leading from the highway to the commune; she would only allow the doctor to view the body. After checking the corpse and returning to the nurses, Allen was visibly chuckling, unable to contain his amazement that Marie insisted that Edith emitted a pulse. He convinced Marie to let the nurses check, and they too detected not even a flutter from Edith's wrist. Young would later recall of Marie's nurses and followers:

> *We found the two nurses had everything well in hand. Twice a day they gave the patient a salt bath, and a milk enema. The milk was to give her nourishment and replace the dead cells in the live tissue, and the salt baths kept her clean, and well preserved. The nurses instructed us to press our fingers in the soles of the patient's feet, and when we could not detect any pulse they had us press our fingers on the crown of her head. Since we*

could not find a pulse the nurses determined we did not have a sixth sense, something they professed to have. Dorothy and I were not fooled. We knew poor Mrs. Peshak was a corpse, well preserved and very clean. She has skin stretched over small bones with no muscle or fat, as she had died of cancer, no telling how long ago. However, there definitely was no public health hazard, so we drove away exited [sic] *over what we had seen. How the two nurses were so duped we could never figure out.*

Dr. Allen and the nurses decided that Edith's mummified corpse posed no threat to public health and that, for the time being, they would leave the colony with its corpse. For the next year and a half, the rituals would be continued as Elmer prayed over his wife's body, believing that he was not a widower but rather a married man awaiting his wife's return to the mortal world. Over the period between the summer of 1936 and the entirety of 1937, the press caught wind of the story of the mummified Edith. A large portion of the nation's citizens were outraged. Anger over the situation in San Juan County became increasingly hard to manage. When Marie said that she would once again resurrect Edith, the local authorities reinvolved themselves in the issue of Edith's remains. They insisted on a death certificate, which Marie refused to provide, especially in late April or early May 1937, when Frank C. Peshak, Edith and Elmer's son, demanded they do something about retrieving his mother's body.

Because of the public's interest in the unbelievable situation in Utah, attorney Adams found himself once more traveling to the Home of Truth. Yet unbeknownst to the authorities, reporter Jack Dewitt had interviewed Ogden that May and learned that her followers had placed Edith's body in a large crevice located at the base of a cliff behind the colony and closed it off with a large rock. However, Adams did not completely believe them, as a former member of the commune, Thomas F. Robertson, submitted an affidavit swearing that Marie Ogden, acting as leader of the community, ordered him to take the body from the small cave, and when Elmer Peshak was away from the settlement, he built a large pyre in a creek washout and burned her corpse on the fire while Marie watched. Marie informed Elmer that her body had been "spirited away" to keep it from "curious and prying eyes." To further complicate the matter, Jack Dewitt claimed that Edith's body had only been partially burnt because he snuck onto the grounds, up to the rock crevice and moved the stone to reveal a half-charred corpse before him.

Whatever the state of Edith's remains, her death certificate was officially signed by Marie Ogden and Elmer Peshak on May 4, 1937. Marie signed the document as the undertaker and Elmer as the informant. On the section of the form asking whether remains have been buried, cremated or removed, Marie crossed out these options and wrote in "Disintegration of body." Twelve members of the Home of Truth community are all that remained from the one hundred followers Marie could count in 1935; the stress of having their community always in the newspapers and Marie being unable to resurrect Edith finally convinced people to flee the commune. Marie continued the Home of Truth late into the 1940s, giving up on the *San Juan Record* in 1949 and retiring to live in quiet solitude with her follower and partner, A.D. Miller. Marie Ogden died in a senior home in Blanding, Utah. She was not buried with her last remaining followers interred in the Home of Truth Cemetery. After her death, the few followers she maintained, even into the 1970s, burned her personal and professional papers to save her secrets from public attention. Elmer Peshak died in early April 1949; his body was returned to Boise for burial at Morris Hill Cemetery next to his son Frank, having died in 1946. A plaque honoring Edith rests next to those of her husband and son, but what exactly lies beneath it?

WHERE TO FIND EDITH: What was left of Edith Peshak now lies in Section N of Morris Hill Cemetery next to Elmer. A few of the ruins of the Home of Truth still stand off Highway 191 and down Route 211 in San Juan County, Utah. The turn onto Route 211 is located almost directly across from the amazing natural monument Church Rock. Up against the hills behind the compound sits a small cemetery for the few members who stayed on. Four visible grave stones, an old gate and a fence are all that remain.

THE OTHER EASTMAN FIRE

Many people who grew up in Boise before the 1980s fondly remember the Eastman Building, standing six stories tall at the corner of Eighth and Main Streets. Throughout the years, the Eastman building played host to many department stores, candy stores and doctors' offices. The Eastman family first arrived in Idaho in 1864, when Mensa and Hosea decided to drive a small herd of cattle from Oregon to sell in the Owyhee mining district. By the time the brothers reached Silver City, all of their cattle had been driven off and stolen by natives, and they were left with just two dollars in their pockets. After a few years of gold mining, the brothers possessed the means to purchase and improve the Idaho Hotel in Silver City. In 1877, Hosea, his business partner Tim Regan and their young wives moved to Boise, while Mensa stayed in Silver City to manage their interests. Hosea and Tim purchased the Overland Hotel, a landmark on the Oregon Trail, located at Eighth and Main in Boise. Hosea's sons Frank and Ben, who were both born in the Overland, would go on to replace the dilapidated hotel with the Overland Office Building, also known as the Eastman Building, in 1905. In 1987, many Boiseans who worked their first jobs or had their first dates in the iconic building watched it go up in flames in a fire that completely gutted the structure, ending the Eastman legacy in Boise. The lot on which the building stood sat empty for years. Failed developments on the site led to its nickname of the "Boise Hole" until the Zion Bank Building was finally erected. However, there was another fire in a building owned by the Eastmans predating the fire at the Eastman Building downtown, an inferno more devastating to the members of the family themselves.

Left: Edith Eastman and children. *Harold Sigler Collection, Idaho State Archives.*

Right: "Children of Ben Eastman." *Harold Sigler Collection. Idaho State Archives.*

The home that Hosea Eastman had built at 1215 Warm Springs Avenue was a grand structure. Designed by John Paulsen, the same man who was hired by the Eastmans to design the Boise Natatorium and city hall, the home had twenty-six rooms, making it the largest residence in Boise. The mansion was large enough to house Hosea's children and grandchildren, including Frank Jr., who was born two months after his father was killed in an automobile accident in Ontario, Oregon. In 1920, Hosea died at age eighty-four of a cerebral hemorrhage in the Eastman home. Twenty-five years later, Hosea's son Ben followed him to the grave in the same bedroom in which his father passed. This left Ben's wife, Mrs. Edith K. Eastman, alone in the family's mansion.

On the evening of February 17, 1956, an orange glow could be seen coming from the east side of the city. Neighbors who went to investigate found that the Eastman Mansion was engulfed in flames. Hundreds of people gathered to watch the city's fire department battle the blaze for hours. Friends of Edith tried to figure out if she was in the home or if she had gone out for the evening. The fire burned so hotly that it prevented firefighters from entering the structure for some time. When the fire was contained enough to enter the home, they found Edith on the floor in the dining room.

Investigators believed that sparks from the fireplace ignited Edith's clothing and that she died trying to put out the blaze that consumed her entire home. An autopsy confirmed that Edith had died from asphyxiation. Edith was the last person to bear the name of one of the most prominent families to ever settle in Boise.

Where to See It: Sadly, little evidence remains of the once great Eastman family. The home that currently stands at 1215 Warm Springs Avenue was moved there from Idaho Street to make room for a St. Luke's expansion. The sandstone wall that surrounded the Eastman Mansion is the only thing left visible.

THE CAT HUNT

Cats can be noise-making nuisances at times, there's no doubt about it. This is especially true when frisky felines are feral and full of summer passion. Over the spring and summer months of 1871, the back alleys and outskirts of early Boise City resounded with the strange yowls and unearthly hissings of thousands of lustful beasts; the citizens of Boise refused to tolerate the pests any longer. On July 1, 1871, the *Idaho Daily Statesman* reported that a strange competition would be held that Saturday night at 8:30 p.m. That coming Saturday, the "Skimmerhorn Boys" organized two groups of men, hundreds strong, into two different skirmish lines armed with cudgels, pack animals, sacks, blue-red rockets, noise makers, anvils and hammers—all meant to herd the unfortunate cats to two selected sites, where they would be bludgeoned.

One group of men headed south and across the river to Jacob's Mill, while the others traveled east to the assayer's office, located at 210 Main Street. Owners of house cats were advised by the *Daily Statesman* to provide the name of their pets to the organized mob and to keep them indoors. The first team to kill 1,500 cats—none under one year of age, mind you—would be declared the "winner." The cat hunt committee, and there really was one, declared that no more than 3,000 cats should be slaughtered, lest there be a scarcity of game for the next round of hunts, an event held annually; in this case, it was arranged with more regularity due to the large number of cats infesting Boise at that time. After a winner was declared, a feast and ball were held in celebration of the successful roundup; we hope they did not eat

"Boise Flour Mills—Cyrus Jacobs Flour Mill & Brewery." *Jess A. Whitker Collection. Idaho State Archives.*

"Boise Public Buildings—Assay Office ca 1884." *History of Idaho Territory Collection, Idaho State Archives.*

the game they caught. The entry price was a mere three processed cat pelts and a jar of tallow, in this case rendered cat fat. Lest you think this a wholly brutal and backward affair, the pelts and processed fat went to charity. The poor of Boise City were cold and needed coats and candles, making the cat hunt, in reality, an act of philanthropy to some.

WHERE TO SEE IT: The Boise City Assayer's Office building is located at 210 Main Street surrounded by a quiet and tranquil park. Of Jacob's Mill, there is nothing left. It once sat on the southwest corner of the intersection at Fourteenth and Idaho.

BIBLIOGRAPHY

Ada County v. Gilbert, 1894. AR 202, Box 13, Folder 13, Ada County District and Justice Courts Collection, 1864–1922. Idaho State Archives. Boise, Idaho, United States.
American Civil War Research Database. Historical Data Systems Inc., Duxbury, MA.
Boise City Democrat. "A Card." 1884.
Bristol, Sherlock. *Idaho Nomenclature.* Ventura, CA, 1880.
Butte (MT) Miner. "King of Con Men, Taken by Death, Was Known Here." May 1, 1922, 2.
Caldwell Tribune. "First Fatal Accident on the Interurban." March 18, 1910, 3.
———. "Gilbert Discharged." July 28, 1894.
———. "Jimmie Turner, A Gambler Was Fatally Shot." July 21, 1894.
———. "Jimmy Turner Stabbed." April 2, 1892.
———. "Too Quick with a Gun, Billy Gilbert Dropped a Man Who Wanted to Kill Him." July 25, 1894.
Corvallis Gazette-Times. "Administrator's Sale of Real Estate." September 28, 1867.
———. "The Insane Man." May 18, 1867, 2.
Corvallis Times. "Circuit Court." January 21, 1870, 3.
D'Easum, Dick. "Outlaws Lost Malad Siege." *Idaho Statesman*, January 31, 1971, 43.

Bibliography

———. "Taps for Two at Boise Barracks." *Idaho Sunday Statesman*, December 7, 1958.
———. "Three Bad Men on the Malad." *Idaho Sunday Statesman*, September 22, 1957, 4.
Dillion, Wilda Collier. *Deaths and Burials: Boise Barracks Military Reserve, Idaho, 1863–1913*. United States: self-published, 2003.
El Paso Times. "A Gambler Shot." July 20, 1894.
Evening Capital News. "Sheehan Is Found Guilty by Jury." October 3, 1916, 8.
Helena Weekly Herald. "Maroni Hicks." December 18, 1879, 8.
Idaho Daily Statesman. "Accident Version Given." February 23, 1922, 7.
———. "Accident Victims Improve." June 4, 1924, 6.
———. "Advertisement." June 26, 1894.
———. "Big Orchard. Sheriff Robbins Returns Empty." September 5, 1889, 3.
———. "Body of Tommy Watkins Found." June 22, 1903, 5.
———. "Bond to Hang on April 14." February 19, 1905, 1.
———. "Brief City News." February 22, 1922, 5.
———. "Brief Local News." August 2, 1909, 2.
———. "Child Suffers Leg Injuries in Elevator." December 14, 1947, 2.
———. "Citizen's Notice." May 5, 1866, 2.
———. "Company Not Responsible. Coroner's Jury Returns Verdict in Railway Accident." March 15, 1910, 5.
———. "Dora Weise Is Dead." November 16, 1917, 8.
———. "Driver Crushed by Freight Elevator." July 30, 1909, 6.
———. "Elevator Collapse Fatal to Boisean." September 4, 1952, 9.
———. "Fall Is Fatal to Boise Boy." December 19, 1926, 1.
———. "A Fatal Accident." April 1, 1892, 8.
———. "For Sale." October 24, 7.
———. "Found Horse and Buggy but No Trace of Bodies." June 5, 1903, 3.
———. "Girl Injured in Elevator." November 17, 1917, 1.
———. "Henry Neuebaumer Shoots Four People and Suicides." January 23, 1906, 1–3.
———. "Hold Grant Ward Services Monday." December 21, 1926, 5.
———. "Home of First Fruit Drier Stands on Warm Springs." September 22, 1941, 4.
———. "Idaho Pioneer Is Victim of Accident. Charles Villeneuve Instantly Killed on Boise & Interurban Line." March 12, 1910, 1.
———. "Injured Workers Resting Easily." June 3, 1924, 2.

BIBLIOGRAPHY

———. "Jim Turner Stabbed, an Unpleasant Outcome of a Sunday Row." March 28, 1892.

———. "Jimmy Turner Killed, Shot to Death by Billy Gilbert at the Free Roll." July 19, 1894.

———. "Jimmy Turner's Arrest, He Struck a Woman then He Went to Jail." November 28, 1891.

———. "John Konopeck." May 20, 1869, 2.

———. June 26, 1921, 18.

———. "Local Brevities." December 5, 1893.

———. "Local Brevities." July 26, 1894, 1.

———. "Local Brevities." November 26, 1891.

———. "Lost His Arm. Elmer Morrison Meets with a Distressing Accident." November 30, 1893.

———. "Move Military Cemetery." April 26, 1907.

———. "Mrs. Eastman Dies in Residence Fire." February 18, 1956, 1.

———. "Murdered in His Own Home." October 7, 1904, 3.

———. "Neuebaumer Left Buried Gold Dust." January 27, 1906, 3.

———. "Obituary Notice." May 22, 1869, 3.

———. "Pioneers' Graves to Be Moved." April 13, 1909, 5.

———. "Prominent Real Estate Man Drowned at Natatorium." February 8, 1908, 2.

———. "Religious Cult Awaits Revival of Dead Woman." February 27, 1937, 12.

———. "Romance Lurks Among the Graves of Boise's Neglected First City of the Dead." May 6, 1907.

———. "Sawmill Accident. Elmer Morrison, the Victim." December 1, 1893.

———. "Services Arranged for Albert Call." September 5, 1952, 11.

———. "Sewell's Condition Improves." July 31, 1909, 2.

———. "Silent Camp, New Soldier Plot Has Burial." May 12, 1913, 10.

———. "Son Asks Utah to Fight Cult." May 1, 1937, 1.

———. "Strange Cult Hides Shrine." July 7, 1936, 1.

———. "Two Helpless Children Drowned in the River." June 4, 1903, 1.

———. "Utah Cult Refuses to Bury Dead Woman in Belief She Will Be Resurrected." November 23, 1935, 2.

———. "Widow Held as Accomplice." October 5, 1904, 1.

———. "Wieser Bridge." October 24, 1903, 5.

———. "Woman Dies from Effects of Burns. Mrs. W.G. Stone Succumbs to Her Injuries." October 6, 1905, 3.

BIBLIOGRAPHY

———. "Woman Saved From Horrible Fate by Rolling in a Ditch" September 17, 1905, 6.

———. "Worry About the Graves." March 13, 1912.

Idaho Semi-Weekly World. "Wilson Still at Large." October 29, 1880, 3.

Idaho Statesman. "'Doc' Sheehan Injured." October 17, 1915, 5.

———. "Identity of Body Found in Church Sought." December 7, 1982, 32.

———. "Jury Taps Five Kegs and Sips." October 1, 1916, 5.

———. "Little Headway in Probe into Arson Case." March 10, 1914, 6.

———. "Rooming Houses Are Raided by Detectives." September 27, 1915, 6.

———. "Story of Wonderful Bunco Game Revived When Principal Actor Is Cinched for Term in Prison." August 3, 1919, 10.

———. "Suicide Victim in Church Died of Cyanide Poisoning." December 16, 1982, 40.

———. "Tree-Lined River Welcome Oasis to Trappers, Modern Travelers." June 18, 1965, 60.

Idaho Sunday Statesman. "The Board Had a Meeting." June 11, 1967, 36.

———. "Mr. J.S. White." November 6, 1955, 37.

———. "Saws of Old Boise Log Mill Hummed During Civil War." October 13, 1940.

Idaho Tri-Weekly Statesman. "Ada County Volunteers." March 22, 1866.

———. "Another Chapter of Crime." April 5, 1866.

———. "Another Terrible Tragedy. A Man's Entrails Cut Out." November 3, 1870, 3.

———. "Anthony McBride." August 20, 1867, 3.

———. "Bad Egg." July 17, 1884, 3.

———. "Blake." November 15, 1870, 2.

———. "Body of Dr. McIteeny Found." August 9, 1866.

———. "The Burmester Trial." December 28, 1869, 2.

———. "The Burmester Trial." December 25, 1869, 2.

———. "The Burmester Trial." December 23, 1869, 2.

———. "The Burmester Trial." January 28, 1870, 2.

———. "The Capture of the Escaped Convicts Mays." October 26, 1880, 3.

———. "The Case of Litell." August 10, 1869, 1.

———. "Cheerful Conversation." January 14, 1868, 3.

———. "City Cemetery." April 6, 1869, 2.

———. "Death Notices." September 16, 1869.

———. "Description of the Escaped Convicts." September 25, 1880, 3.

———. "District Court Proceedings." December 27, 1875, 3.
———. "The Escaped Convicts." October 19, 1880, 3.
———. "The Escaped Convicts." October 2, 1880, 3.
———. "The Escaped Convicts." September 28, 1880, 3.
———. "Execution of McBride." January 25, 1868, 3.
———. "The Graveyard." October 23, 1866, 2.
———. "High Water." May 16, 1876, 3.
———. "Jail Delivery." September 25, 1880, 3.
———. "Jewish Cemetery." April 29, 1869.
———. July 1, 1871, 3.
———. "The Late Homicide." September 16, 1869.
———. "Meeting of the Boise Volunteers." February 27, 1866.
———. "Meeting of the Citizen's of Boise City." February 24, 1866.
———. "Mr. T.J. Forster of Fort McKinley." December 23, 1880, 3.
———. "Mrs. Blake." November 5, 1870, 3.
———. "A New Indian Raid." February 17, 1866.
———. "Our Cemetery Grounds." July 9, 1872.
———. "Paracide." February 5, 1867, 2.
———. "Prisoner Escaped." November 19, 1867, 2.
———. "Sentenced," August 30, 1867, 3.
———. "Still at Large." October 9, 1880, 3.
———. "Volunteers Gone." March 3, 1866.
Idaho World. "Execution of Simeon Walters." December 16, 1869, 1.
———. "Failed to Indict." November 18, 1869.
———. "The Litell Case." Aug 12, 1869, 2.
———. "The Trial of Simeon Walters." March 18, 1869, 1.
Illustrated Police News. February 16, 1884.
Kemp, Emma. "The Disembodied Word: Marie Ogden's Home of Truth." Otis College of Art & Design, 2016.
McClure, Erin. "A Capitol Tragedy: Idaho History that Hits Home." *Boise State Public Radio*, 2017. https://www.boisestatepublicradio.org/post/capitol-tragedy-idaho-history-hits-home#stream/0.
McConnell, William John. *Early History of Idaho*. Caldwell, ID: Caxton Printers, 1913.
McConnell, William John, and Howard R. Driggs. *Frontier Law: A Story of Vigilante Days*. Yonkers-on-Hudson, NY: World Book, 1926.
Montana Post. "Idaho." February 23, 1867, 4.
NamUs. "Unidentified Person / NamUs #UP57814." April, 12, 2021. https://namus.nij.ojp.gov/case/UP57814.

BIBLIOGRAPHY

National Archives and Records Administration (NARA), Washington, D.C. Returns from Regular Army Infantry Regiments, June 1821–December 1916; Microfilm Serial: M665; Roll: 154.

———. NAI Title: U.S., Civil War Pension Index: General Index to Pension Files, 1861–1934; NAI Number: T288; Record Group Title: Records of the Department of Veterans Affairs, 1773–2007; Record Group Number: 15; Series Title: U.S., Civil War Pension Index: General Index to Pension Files, 1861–1934; Series Number: T288; Roll: 293.

National Park Service. "U.S., Civil War Soldiers, 1861–1865." Database online. Provo, UT: Ancestry.com Operations Inc., 2007.

Ogden Standard Examiner. "Body Reposes Four Months in Cult Home." June 12, 1935, 3.

Ogden, Marie. "Mrs. Marie Ogden and the Home of Truth." Interview by Hector Lee. Utah Humanities Research Foundation, March 5, 1946.

Omaha Evening Bee-News. "Cult Awaiting Resurrection of Woman Dead Nearly a Year." December 29, 1935, 38.

Owyhee Semi-Weekly Tidal Wave. "The Killing of Sergeant Vogel." September 23, 1869.

Post-Register. "Civilization Due to Fall." October 29, 1936, 18.

———. "Explains Resurrection Hopes." May 7, 1937, 8.

———. "Utahn Denies Pelley Charge." February 13, 1940, 1.

———. "Utah 'Resurrection Case' Nears Close." May 4, 1937, 3.

———. "Utah 'Resurrection Case' Reaches Dramatic Climax." May 4, 1937, 1.

Record-Union. "A Reward of $2,000." April 17, 1883, 1.

Rhodenbaugh, Harold. "It Won Prizes at World's Fairs." *Idaho Sunday Statesman,* November 25, 1928, 18.

Royal Cornwall Gazette. "Dreadful Outrage on a Lady." July 3, 1869, 6.

Salt Lake Herald. "Maroni Hicks." January 4, 1880, 3.

Salt Lake Telegram. "Cult Leader Defies State Probers." April 28, 1937, 1.

San Francisco Chronicle. "Fatal Saloon Fight, Shooting of a Well-Known Montana Sporting Man." July 20, 1894.

Sketches of the Inter-Mountain States: Together with Biographies of Many Prominent and Progressive Citizens Who Have Helped in the Development and History-Making of This Marvelous Region: 1847–1909: Utah, Idaho, Nevada. Salt Lake City, UT, 1909.

Supreme Court of Idaho. *State of Idaho v. Thomas Eugene Creech*, September 21, 1983. Accessible via FindLaw, https://caselaw.findlaw.com/id-supreme-court/1447835.html.

Terhune, Katie. "Former Boise Priest Convicted in Brutal Child Porn Case Dies in Prison." KTVB, October 20, 2020. https://www.ktvb.com/article/news/crime/boise-father-faucher-child-porn-priest-dies-in-prison/277-56642caf-894b-4731-98ca-e697527e6ddd.

Thayne, Stanley J. "The Home of Truth: The Metaphysical World of Marie Ogden." PhD. diss. Brigham Young University, 2009.

U.S. Census Bureau. 1870 Federal Census. Accessed via Ancestry.com.

Valle, Doris. "The Home of Truth." *San Juan Record*, June 2, 2004, 20. Accessed via newspapers.com.

Wade, J.D. *Brave as a Lion: Jeff Standifer and the Knights of the Golden Circle*. N.p.: Amazon KDP, 2019.

ABOUT THE AUTHORS

Amanda Smith, IdaHistory Collection.

MARK IVERSON grew up in Seattle, Washington, where he followed bands like Soundgarden and Alice in Chains. Mark joined the Peace Corps and spent time in the Balkans. He moved to Idaho in 2009 and founded IdaHistory in 2019. He earned his master's degree in history from BSU. He is a huge rock music fan and collects vintage Star Wars toys that he tells his children not to touch.

JEFF WADE was born here in the greatest state of the Union. He holds a B.S. in criminal justice and has worked in public service for almost thirteen years. He published his first book, *Brave as a Lion: Jeff Standifer and the Knights of the Golden Circle*, in December 2019 and was the creator, co-host and producer of *Cascadia Podcast: History of the Pacific Northwest*. He loves metal and can't get much work done without listening to it.

Learn about their local walking tours, research services and more at www.idahistory.com.